SMALL GROUP BIBLE STUDIES

HOW TO
LEAD
THEM

SMALL GROUP BIBLE STUDIES

HOW TO LEAD THEM

PAT J. SIKORA

STANDARD
PUBLISHING
Cincinnati, Ohio

Library of Congress Cataloging-in-Publication Data

Sikora, Pat J.
   Small group Bible studies / Pat J. Sikora
      p. cm.
   Includes bibliographical references and index.
   Contents: [1] How to lead them.
   ISBN 0-87403-858-8 (v. 1)
   1. Bible—Study. 2. Bible—Study—Textbooks. 3. Church
group work. I. Title.
BS600.2.S55 1991
268'.6—dc20   91-9773
                                          CIP

Lovingly dedicated to Dr. Bob and Gudren Noonan, **Dedication**
who devoted so many years of their lives to the
training of discussion and small group leaders through
the Careers ministry in Palo Alto, San Francisco, and
elsewhere in the Bay Area. Your influence, which was
the beginning of my interest in small groups, is seen
throughout this book.

Acknowledgments

I am grateful to many who helped to make this book possible. Bob and Gudren Noonan not only taught me much of what is in this book, but also reviewed the manuscript and made many helpful suggestions. I am particularly indebted to them for many of the suggestions in Chapter 7, "Why Didn't You Warn Me?"

In addition, I'm grateful for the manuscript reviews, comments, and suggestions of several colleagues and friends:

Rev. John Payton, Th.D. (pastor, First Church of the Nazarene of San Luis Obispo, CA) and his wife Jadene provided excellent comments on the usefulness of the book for new small group leaders.

Rev. Robert Mayer, M.A. (Director of Publications for the Adventist Christian General Conference) contributed technical, theological, and experiential insights.

John Dillman, M.Div. (staff to San Francisco Careers) supplied wonderful comments based on years of experience, as well as excellent copyediting.

Mark Mitchell, M.A. (pastor of small group

ministries at Central Peninsula Church, Foster City, CA) shared a wealth of small group experience and training. Tina Torres, my friend and a former small group Bible study leader, offered her excellent editing skills, insights, and prayer support.

Jonathan Arnold, Ph.D. provided his professional insights for the section on dealing with the emotionally disturbed person.

Ken and Carla Claar, owners of The Door Christian Bookstore in San Carlos, CA, for their assistance with the "Resources for Leaders" appendix.

My thanks to Cindy Peterson, my friend and a member of the Moms' Bible Study, who labored long hours in word processing.

And a very special thanks to my dear friends, Ruth Raimer and Kaja Berenberg, who prayed without ceasing and provided loving and fun care for Joshua while I labored day after day to complete this book. Another special thank-you to my husband Bob, who picked up the load so I could write. And thanks to the many others who prayed and encouraged me. Each of you has a special place in my heart and in this book.

Contents

INTRODUCTION

You Can Do It!

I BELIEVE IN Bible study. I believe in small groups. And I believe that almost any Christian can become an effective leader of a small group Bible study. That's why I've written this book —to help you become a leader or a more capable leader. With that as my premise, I've designed it for two specific audiences.

First, this book is for the person who has never led a small group Bible study. Perhaps you've seen a need in your church, your neighborhood, your work place, or among your friends. You've never led a group, but think you might like to try it. Or perhaps you've never considered leading a Bible study, but someone in leadership in your church or Christian organization has invited you to try this new ministry. Maybe you'll lead a small independent group. Or you may lead one of several small groups within a larger ministry. Either way, this book offers all you need to know to get started and to grow as a leader. It's your own personal training session, covering all the topics I'd include in preparing new leaders in the various Bible studies I've led. If you find the book overwhelming at first, read the rest of this section, then skim the Table of Contents. Start where your interests or needs are. As you're comfortable with one section, move on to the next.

Second, this handbook is for the experienced leader who wants to improve his skills or learn to deal with specific problems in a group. Perhaps you've been leading a group for a while, but don't feel as confident as you'd like to. Perhaps your group has a chronic talker or someone who won't talk at all. Perhaps you're dealing with non-Christians who ask tough questions. You'll find the answers you need in this handbook. Use it as a reference book to help you deal with specific problems. Review it quickly before you begin a new group. Consider it a refresher course.

Now, I know that if you're a Bible study leader, you're a busy person. You don't want to wade through pages of prose to find the help you need. That's why the format is simple and conversational, flavored with true anecdotes (although in some cases I've changed names and details to protect the privacy of others).

Here's a chapter-by-chapter overview so you'll know where you're going.

Chapter 1, "From Here to Maturity," gives the six key components of effective small group Bible studies. The rest of the book will build on these components to show you specifically how to form and lead a group.

Chapter 2, "Who Me? A Leader?" identifies eight qualities of leadership. That will help you assess your readiness to lead a group, as well as to assess any helpers or additional leaders you might need.

In Chapter 3, "Keys to Changed Lives," we'll discuss seven essential elements that every small group Bible study should include.

"All of our theology must eventually become biography. The constant challenge in this life we call Christian is the translation of all we believe to be true into our day-to-day life-style."
—Tim Hansel, *You Gotta Keep Dancin'*

Chapter 4, "Learning by the Book," gives recommendations for evaluating and selecting study guides for use in small group Bible study.

Chapter 5, "Before You Begin," lists seven preliminaries you should consider before beginning your group.

Then in Chapter 6, "Hey! I'm a Leader!" we'll discuss that very important first meeting and four principles for leading a good discussion group.

And Chapter 7, "Why Didn't You Warn Me?" focuses on 19 potential problems and how to solve them. This chapter is particularly helpful for experienced leaders, but even the beginner will learn a great deal from it.

Finally, the Appendixes provide lots of additional practical information for your use, such as a resource list, get-acquainted activities, lesson planning sheets, and a sample evaluation form.

Throughout the book I made one assumption: the reason people join and remain in a small group Bible study is to grow spiritually. Yes, the fellowship is rewarding. Being part of a group is fun. But our purpose as leaders must be to encourage measurable, visible spiritual growth in each person in our group. Our goal is to see lives transformed. So, let's get started.

"Small groups are not simply a program for the church. They are a way of being the church. I am convinced that without intentional Christian community, we cannot be the people of God for each other and to the world as God intended."
—Roberta Hestenes

CHAPTER 1

From Here to Maturity

IN THE INTRODUCTION we suggested that the goal of any small group Bible study is growth—measurable, visible spiritual growth for each person in our group. The product of spiritual growth is maturity. That's what we're aiming for.

We find a good definition of maturity in Ephesians 4:12-15. In the verses immediately preceding this passage, the apostle Paul told the Ephesians that God had placed within their church (and all others) various leaders who share one specific responsibility: "to prepare God's people for works of service, so that the body of Christ may be built up until we all reach unity in the faith and in the knowledge of the Son of God and become mature, attaining to the whole measure of the fullness of Christ" (Ephesians 4:12, 13).

"Until we all reach unity in the faith and in the knowledge of the Son of God and become mature, attaining to the whole measure of the fullness of Christ" (Ephesians 4:13).

The Greek word for "mature" is *teleios*. It means "whole, complete, or undivided." Paul further defines what he means in the next two verses as he gives us a yardstick for measuring our success: "Then we will no longer be infants, tossed back and forth by the waves, and blown here and there by every wind of teaching and by the cunning and craftiness of men in their deceitful scheming. Instead, speaking the truth in love, we will in all things grow up into him who is the Head, that is, Christ" (Ephesians 4:14, 15).

When we work with people in a small group Bible study, then, our goal is to develop mature people who 1) understand the Word of God; 2) can distinguish truth from error; and 3) can apply its truths to all areas of their lives. We want to develop people who are "grown up" in their faith. Let's look at some specific ways to accomplish that goal.

"Please be patient. God isn't finished with me yet." —Inter-Varsity Graffito

The Six Components

✳

"Do your best to present yourself to God as one approved, a workman who does not need to be ashamed and who correctly handles the word of truth" (2 Timothy 2:15).

When we talk about a "small group Bible study," it's likely that each person has his or her own ideas about what that means. Your understanding of the term will be based primarily on your own experience or on the experiences of others you know.

It's true there are many models for small groups. Nowhere in Scripture will you find a clear definition of exactly what such a group must include. Indeed, any models of groups in Bible times reflect the culture and needs of those people, just as our groups must reflect our culture and needs. That gives us some freedom to design groups that will most effectively encourage maximum spiritual growth.

I've participated in small groups of various types for over 14 years; my husband Bob has had even more experience. Together or individually we've led many groups and assisted with others. And sometimes we've simply been participants. Some groups have been Bible studies; others have been based on books or the leader's expertise. Some have addressed specific needs; others have been general in nature. We've been in women's or men's groups and mixed groups. Some groups have caused each of us to make gigantic spiritual strides; others have been pleasant, but haven't contributed much to our maturity. From these experiences we've gleaned six key components that yield maximum growth for participants in small groups.

Component 1: Facilitate, Don't Teach

In the Introduction to this book I made a daring statement. I said I believe that almost any Christian can become an effective leader of a small group Bible study. If you're like many people considering leadership, that statement raised a red flag in your mind. But still I believe it. Let me explain.

I didn't say that any Christian can be an effective Bible *teacher.* And let's face it, that's what many of us think of when we think of a Bible study: there's this expert standing in front of the group communicating pearls of wisdom from the Greek or Hebrew text laced with appropriate anecdotes, and of course, the inevitable three points. Most of us can't do that. It's a gift, most often combined with years of study.

But I said that any Christian can become a small group Bible study *leader.* This method does not require a teaching leader, but rather a *facilitator,* a fellow struggler in life. We don't expect him or her to have all the answers. Rather, this person is committed to helping each group member to become conformed to the image of Jesus Christ through the study of the Word.

Remember that God's Word achieves its life-changing effect on people through the ministry of the Holy Spirit—not through your skills. The effective group leader acts as a moderator and a guide, not as an authority or a teacher. He allows the Bible to be the group's authority and the Holy Spirit to be their

An effective group can take many forms. It may be a Sunday-school class, a mixed group, a men's or women's study, an evangelistic study, or a discipleship group. Within the six components you have a lot of room for individuality.

teacher. This guideline is essential in understanding everything else in this book.

Component 2: Keep It Small

It's rather obvious, but some people do miss the point. A small group needs to be small.

That concept is appalling to us Westerners—even in the church—who often measure success by size. We're delighted when our churches or groups grow. We like to boast about how many people we're ministering to. But the fact remains: to be most effective, a group needs to be small. The reason is that it's impossible to be intimate with more than a few people.

Jesus gave us a perfect example. He chose a group of twelve men to study with Him. Yes, He had thousands who followed Him and loved to hear Him teach. And yes, He gave a significant amount of time to the multitudes. But His closest relationships, His friends, His disciples, numbered only twelve. These men were privy to His innermost thoughts, His struggles, His prayers, and His confidences. He taught them, held them accountable for growth, commissioned them in ministry, and loved them even when they failed.

Using the biblical model, many small group leaders suggest twelve is an optimum number. For me, it's an absolute maximum. I prefer groups of six to eight members. Why?

The main reason is time. If we could spend all day every day together, as Jesus did with His disciples, twelve would be fine. But most of us can't do that. We simply don't have that luxury. We have jobs, families, and other responsibilities. If we're lucky we get a couple of hours per week together as a group. Therefore, we need a number that is manageable within the context of our lives.

I use four questions to determine how many to include in my groups.

First, *how often and for how long will the group meet?* Most small groups meet either weekly or every other week for one-and-one-half to two-and-one-half hours. That's not very long to develop committed, accountable relationships. The more people in your group, the more frequently you'll need to meet, or the longer your meeting time must be.

What are the attendance requirements of the group? The stronger the requirement for regular attendance, the more people will be present at each meeting. It's difficult for everyone to participate actively in a two-hour meeting if there are more than six or seven people present. Discussing study responses and sharing prayer needs both get out of hand—or they are shortened until they're meaningless.

Regardless of the requirements, what are the attendance realities of this group? Unfortunately some people never get emotionally committed to a group. They won't make extreme efforts to attend. If something better comes along, they're gone. Others, like mothers of young children or busy executives, find that life comes crashing in. They're simply unable to attend every meeting. While you'll want to stress the importance of regular attendance, the reality is that, in many of our groups, a bit of grace will be necessary.

How many dropouts do you expect? Most people begin with the best of intentions, but some will never become committed members of your group. People leave groups for any number of reasons. Some find that the study or the group isn't what they expected. Others lose interest. Some people move or get promoted. Others face major changes in their lives. Whatever the reason, it's rare to end with exactly the same group you began with. In fact, in over 14 years of leading groups, I've only had that happen twice!

You'll never be able to predict with absolute certainty how many you'll lose from your group, but give it your best estimate. You can start with a slightly larger group than you ultimately want, but don't overestimate. Otherwise, you'll find people dropping out due to dissatisfaction with the group. So, for the most effective group, seek a maximum of twelve, and an ideal of six to eight members.

Divide and conquer. Now you see the wisdom in keeping your group small. But what happens when you have more than eight (or even twelve) people who want to be part of your group? That's simple. You split into an appropriate number of smaller groups, pray for more leadership, and begin training new leaders by sharing the resources you've found helpful. Sometimes you can plan for this division; sometimes you're caught off guard.

When I started a Bible study for mothers at our church I expected 25 to 30 women to join the first year and planned accordingly. My first task was to recruit two additional leaders and three co-leaders (more about co-leaders later). I also identified several women I considered potential leaders, with the idea of using them to start new groups should the demand develop.

To develop unity, the entire group met weekly for worship and announcements and every other week for an expanded application of the study. The Bible study itself, sharing, accountability, and prayer took place in our small groups.

A more spontaneous need occurred the first year John was a leader in his church's men's Bible study. Somehow he was assigned the largest room. Since men could join throughout the year he got most of the newcomers. By the time he had 15 men in his group it was clear that something needed to change.

He had a capable co-leader, Randall, who was willing to take half of the group for the sharing and prayer time. That allowed a bit more intimacy and helped them keep the sharing to a reasonable amount of time. As the group continued to grow, Randall eventually took half of the group for the study portion as well. Although they didn't officially split the group, they accomplished the same goal informally and had much more effective groups as a result.

One key in keeping our groups small is prayer. We need to anticipate the need, then pray that God will raise up the additional leaders we need. And why shouldn't He? He longs for His people to mature. He'll be faithful as we are faithful. In Chapter 2 we'll discuss the qualities of a leader. This will help you not only to measure yourself, but also identify others in your group who would be good leaders.

Component 3:
Foster Commitment to the Group

The third component in creating a small group that will bring people to maturity is commitment to the group. You're not developing a loosely formed congregation, but a small group. What's the difference?

In a group people commit themselves to one another. The most effective groups are those in which the people develop a deep concern and abiding love for one another. They become one in spirit and in purpose. It's almost impossible to plan or orchestrate this commitment through selectivity. Rather, it's the work of the Holy Spirit as each person yields to Him and to the others in the group. Such commitment will result in people sharing not only their lives, but also their resources with one another.

Prepare to be surprised by those God calls you to love. I've often found that the person I like the least in the beginning of a group almost always becomes a good friend as we both open ourselves to one another and the Holy Spirit.

In a group people commit themselves to being open, honest, vulnerable, and accountable. In the type of group we're talking about there's no room for pretense. People must be open and honest with one another. They must take the risk of being vulnerable. Each person also needs to be mutually accountable to and for each member's maturation.

This is never easy. Often it's uncomfortable. Sometimes it's downright unpleasant. But true growth and maturity come most effectively in such a setting. Each person must be willing to do his part.

I've seen it happen many times. The person who joined the group quite reluctantly, warning that she was not willing to share, to pray out loud, or to answer questions soon became one of the most transparent

"Now the body is not made up of one part but of many. . . . But in fact God has arranged the parts in the body, every one of them, just as he wanted them to be" (1 Corinthians 12:14, 18).

members of the group. And not surprisingly, such people also have grown the most through the group.

In a group, people commit themselves to the group. In addition to committing themselves to the individuals within the group, members need to commit themselves to the group itself. Each member must be willing to decrease in individual importance so the group as a whole can increase. Each must be willing to prepare, attend, share, and serve in order for the group to succeed. Such commitment creates synergy, where the whole is greater than the sum of the individual parts. In such a group the maturing process can occur unimpeded. In such a group the Holy Spirit can work unfettered.

Follow me! The leader is essential to helping the group develop cohesiveness. Developing a sense of group is a tall order. How do you accomplish this? First, it's your responsibility as the leader. You must desire the cohesiveness of the group and must diligently give yourself to that goal. What are some keys to accomplishing this?

The leader must create the desire for the group to jell. If you have a ho-hum attitude about the group, you'll have a ho-hum group. If you're excited and enthusiastic about what God is going to do in and through your group, you'll have a dynamic group that results in changed lives. Your attitude is contagious. So if you're feeling ambivalent about the group you're forming, pray that the Lord will revitalize you and fill you with excitement for what He can do in the life of each member.

The leader must set the pace and the example. The members of your group will be watching you, so you must set the pace. If you're sincerely enthusiastic you'll have an enthusiastic group. If you're bored you'll have a bored group. If you're willing to be vulnerable and share deeply most members of your group will follow. If you're willing to be accountable to members of your group they'll be willing to be accountable to you and to one another. So the key is for you to model the behavior you want your group to practice.

The leader must not be afraid to lead. Probably the biggest mistake I've made in leading groups—and I've made it more than once—is my failure to take charge and be the leader. In an effort to encourage others to feel ownership in the group and to avoid appearing bossy, I'm often more lax than I should be. I create a leadership void. I'm slowly learning that when I'm the leader of the group, people expect me to lead.

Of course, this doesn't mean that I should be a dictator demanding to have everything exactly as I want it. It doesn't mean that I don't need anyone else to participate in the decision-making. What it does mean, though, is that I must be willing to take responsibility for the health of the group, even if it means making an unpopular decision. It's a delicate balance, but more people seem to err on the side of weakness than on the side of strength.

See "Get Off That Pedestal!" and "The Leader as a Model" in Chapter 2 for examples and further discussion of this concept.

The best way to lead, then, is to be open and to model vulnerability. Let the members of your group get close enough to see your struggles. Let them get to know you—warts and all. The more human you are, the more credibility you'll have and the more you'll encourage the members of your group to grow.

Component 4: Study God's Word

The fourth component for developing a group that will bring people to maturity is the type of study you choose. Growth occurs when people study the Word of God, not the word of man. The Bible should be our primary source document and our foundation of truth.

There are hundreds of excellent Christian books on the market and more are published every year. Many godly men and women have written about many subjects that each of us needs to study more deeply. And many of these books are now published with study guides so groups just like yours can use them. But as good as they are, these are all the word of man, not the Word of God. The authors may write about the Word, but their books are not the Word. And if they aren't the Word, they don't have the power of the Word.

The writer to the Hebrews exhorts, "The word of God is living and active. Sharper than any double-edged sword, it penetrates even to dividing soul and spirit, joints and marrow; it judges the thoughts and attitudes of the heart" (Hebrews 4:12). That's my goal in leading a group. Personally, I don't have time to do just any study. If I'm going to devote myself to leading a group, I want it to be penetrating and powerful. I want it to divide soul and spirit, separate truth from error. I want it to change people's lives. And I believe the best way to assure that is to study God's message to us—the Bible.

Chapter 4 provides an in-depth discussion on the criteria for selecting a good study guide.

That's not to negate the use of study guides. After all, few of us have time to write our own original studies. But be sure that your study guide requires you to dig into the Bible—not into someone's great prose.

God has promised us, through the prophet Isaiah, "As the heavens are higher than the earth, so are my ways higher than your ways and my thoughts than your thoughts. As the rain and the snow come down from heaven, and do not return to it without watering the earth and making it bud and flourish, so that it yields seed for the sower and bread for the eater, so is my word that goes out from my mouth: It will not return to me empty, but will accomplish what I desire and achieve the purpose for which I sent it" (Isaiah 55:9-11). Do you realize that this guarantee is still in effect today? When we study the Word of God He is intimately present with us, accomplishing His desires and achieving His purpose. How can we ask for more than that?

Component 5:
Require Some Sweat Equity

As a facilitator your goal is to enhance the results of each person's individual study through group interaction. This assumes people must have the materials to do their own personal study before the group meeting.

It assumes regular, individual preparation by each group member before each meeting.

You'll want people to be faithful in doing their assignments. You'll want them to have spent some time and energy integrating the lesson into their lives. Then your job will be easy. They'll have so much to share with one another that your main task will be to keep order!

As your group prepares to do an assignment for the first time, be sure to emphasize that the most effective learning occurs when we allow the Holy Spirit to teach us through our personal study. This means that commentaries and other resources, while valuable, should be the last step in their study rather than the first step.

Component 6: Look for Similar People

A homogeneous group is one composed of people who are similar in several ways. These similarities can encompass any number of characteristics, but generally speaking, the more group members have in common, the more effective the group will be. A homogeneous group will also be easier to lead than a heterogenous group—that is, one made up of dissimilar people. Why? The more people have in common, the more likely they are to bond to one another without a lot of effort. People who are very different have more barriers to overcome; they may have a harder time understanding one another. That isn't to say you *can't* have a group of heterogeneous people. It's just that it takes more work from the leader.

For example, a men's group or a women's group is usually easier to lead and more effective than a couples' group. Many people find it difficult to be open and vulnerable with members of the opposite sex other than their spouses. You'll find that the group jells faster and the sharing and accountability are usually deeper if you don't mix men and women.

The same is true of marrieds and singles, parents and childless adults, or even parents of preschoolers

"All of us are to attain to this *teleios* man of Christlikeness. It does not appear as if Paul [in Ephesians 4:11-16] is giving . . . Christians . . . the option of remaining spiritual children. . . . Whatever Christian maturity is, all Christians are obligated to reach it as quickly as possible and all Christian leaders are obligated to help those sheep under their influence to reach that point."
—Jay Grimstead, *Let's Have a Reformation*

and parents of teens. Many living near the poverty level are uncomfortable with their more affluent neighbors. A well-educated person may find little in common with a group where many haven't graduated from high school.

My husband and I married in our 30's. The Sunday-school class for our age group was full of parents of teens. We weren't even ready for our first child! We found that we were more comfortable, more accepted, and had more in common with the members of the young marrieds. True, they were ten to 15 years younger than we were, but they were in the same "life space." They had all married within the past five years and had no children or very young families. They shared many of our needs and interests.

This is not to say that we want to encourage such barriers in our churches. Nor do we suggest that people should never venture out of the safety of a homogeneous group. But church growth experts and those knowledgeable about small groups have demonstrated that the more people have in common the closer the ties between them. So especially if this is your first time as a leader, look for a group of similar people.

Is It Worth the Effort?

✳

"To this end I labor, struggling with all his energy, which so powerfully works in me" (Colossians 1:29).

Growth. Application. Accountability. Facilitate. Those are frightening words to some. And they sound like work. You may be doubting if you really want to lead a small group Bible study. Will it be worth the effort?

My answer to that question is a resounding yes! I can attest that almost all growth in my Christian life has come as a result of participating in small group Bible studies. And the most significant growth has come when I've served as a leader of such a group.

Others agree that small group Bible studies are essential to growth. For example, the editors at

NavPress say, "Small Bible study groups are one of the most effective tools to help Christians fulfill Christ's great commission to make disciples in every nation."*

What is a disciple? *The American Heritage Dictionary* defines a disciple as "a person who subscribes to the teachings of a master and assists in spreading them." Isn't that what Jesus commanded each of us to do in Matthew 28:19? If we believe that His teachings are true, then we have a responsibility to help others to know them, understand them, and put them into practice in their lives.

And what is our model for this role? Jesus Christ himself. He trained His disciples in a small group. He selected twelve men to walk with Him, talk with Him, watch Him, and learn from Him. He communicated the truth of the Scriptures to them in all they did together. He was committed to them and they were committed to Him and to one another. Was it worth the effort? To answer that question we have only to look at the influence those twelve Galilean peasants have had on the history of the world.

"It all started by Jesus calling a few men to follow Him. This revealed . . . the direction His evangelistic strategy would take. His concern was not with programs to reach the multitudes, but with men whom the multitudes would follow. . . . Men were to be His method of winning the world to God.

"As one might expect, these early efforts . . . had little or no immediate effect upon the religious life of His day, but that did not matter greatly. For . . . these few early converts of the Lord were destined to become the leaders of His church that was to go with the Gospel to the whole world, and from the standpoint of His ultimate purpose, the significance of their lives would be felt throughout eternity. That's the only thing that counts"*

*NavPress, *A Navigator Guide: How to Lead Small Group Bible Studies,* copyright © 1982 by The Navigators, Colorado Springs, CO.

*Robert E. Coleman, *The Master Plan of Evangelism.* Copyright © 1963, 1964 by Robert E. Coleman. Old Tappan, NJ: Revell.

CHAPTER 2

Who, Me? A Leader?

AS WE EXAMINE leadership let's agree that even you can facilitate a discussion—regardless of how shy you are, or how uncertain of yourself. And it doesn't even matter how much biblical or theological training you have or haven't had.

My husband was one of the most introverted people you could imagine when he became a Christian at the age of 28. He wouldn't even talk in class, much less lead anything. After a few months in Careers, an interdenominational singles group in San Francisco, he was invited to become a discussion leader. He panicked. He'd be glad to clean up, but he certainly could never lead a discussion table of eight people! His minister gave him the words of wisdom he needed to try. "Bob," he said, "I know *you* can't lead a discus-

> "Not that we are competent in ourselves to claim anything for ourselves, but our competence comes from God" (2 Corinthians 3:5)

sion. But the Holy Spirit in you can. Give Him a chance to do it."

With fear and trembling Bob gave it a try. He studied. He attended training sessions. He prayed for wisdom and guidance. And he did a good job. Because he allowed the Lord to stretch him, he grew as a Christian and a leader. He's still not comfortable leading Bible studies. But he can do it well because he is open to being God's vessel.

Are you willing to be God's vessel? Are you willing to set aside your fears, your inhibitions, and your pride to learn how to serve the Lord as a small group Bible study leader? Then let's look at some qualities you'll need to develop.

> "The would-be leader of men who affirms and proclaims that he pays no heed to the things of the Spirit is not worthy to lead them." —Miguel de Unamuno

Get Off That Pedestal!

✷

> "The man of integrity walks securely, but he who takes crooked paths will be found out" (Proverbs 10:9).

In today's environment personal integrity is one of the most important qualities a leader can exhibit. Unfortunately it's becoming as rare a commodity within the church of Jesus Christ as it is in the world. What a sad commentary on contemporary Christianity!

The apostle James reminded his readers that those who teach will be judged more strictly (James 3:1). This warning also applies to Bible study leaders or to anyone else who accepts the responsibility of sharing the truths of God with others. It's an awesome responsibility—one not to be taken lightly.

Perhaps the best test of personal integrity is this: Are you the same person in private as you are in public? Are you honest with those you lead? Or do you wear a mask, pretending to be super-spiritual when deep down you know that you're as likely to scream at the kids, kick the dog, or entertain lustful thoughts as the next person?

James also acknowledged that "we all stumble in many ways" (James 3:2). None of us is sinless. We all blow it from time to time. So how can we aspire to the high calling of leadership? I believe there are two cautions which, if taken seriously, will help any leader maintain personal integrity.

First, *avoid the pedestal!* You'll be amazed to discover how the mere act of being the leader will suddenly fill you with all the wisdom of the ages—in the eyes of many in your group or church. Whether you desire it or not, they'll elevate you to the role of expert. It's scary—and it's the reason many of our leaders fall into sin. We aren't perfect and can't expect to be, but in a world that's lacking in heroes, almost anyone will qualify—even you.

"Character is what you are in the dark." —D.L. Moody

When I wrote my first Bible study for our church's women's group I experienced this dilemma. Almost immediately, many in the congregation expected me to know the answer to every theological question. And when I signed with a publisher they were ready to schedule the autograph party! Several said, "We'll be able to say we knew you when . . ." I had to insist that I hadn't changed. I didn't want to be treated like a celebrity, for *my* own good even more than for theirs.

This leads to the second caution. *Begin immediately being open, honest, and vulnerable.* You don't have to have it all together to become a Bible study leader. None of us would qualify if that were true. But it's also unwise to hide your weaknesses as you try to appear more qualified. If you fall into that trap you'll soon begin to believe the lie. You'll live a charade and you'll have a long way to fall when the truth finally comes out. And it will.

I found that as I led more people I needed to be even more open, honest, and vulnerable. I needed to acknowledge that my warts were as ugly as theirs. Of course I still need to use wisdom in deciding how much to share with each person. But I know I'm vulnerable with more people now simply to keep myself honest. I always want to remind members of my groups that they need to follow Jesus Christ, not me. Read 1 Timothy 3:1-7 for some additional thoughts on the personal integrity of a leader. Keep these standards before you as you lead your Bible study.

Give Me a FAT Leader!

❋

"Watch your life and doctrine closely. Persevere in them, because if you do, you will save both yourself and your hearers"
(1 Timothy 4:16)

"Wait a minute!" you say. "What does my weight have to do with leadership?"

Nothing. But it'll sure help you remember three essential qualities in every good leader. FAT is an acronym for Faithful, Available, and Teachable. That's it. You don't have to be a Bible scholar. You needn't have been a Christian for 20 years. You don't even have to have your life perfectly in order. God will begin to use you just as you are, just where you are, if you are simply FAT.

Let's look at these three characteristics and see why they're necessary for successful leadership.

A Leader Must Be Faithful

Faithful applies in two areas. First, *you must be faithful to God and His Word.* That means you must be a Christian. Remember, I've been saying that any *Christian* can become an effective small group leader. If you haven't yet made Jesus Christ the Savior and the Lord of your life, read no further. Run, don't walk, to your minister or to a mature Christian. Ask that person to lead you through the plan of salvation. Then allow God to give you the most important gift you'll ever receive—the gift of eternal life through His Son, Jesus Christ.

If you know beyond a doubt that you are a Christian, "faithful" implies that you must be growing. Do you take time for regular prayer, personal Bible study, and meditation on God's Word? Are you applying what you're learning? Is your goal to become conformed to the image of Jesus Christ? Are you a more faithful Christian today than you were yesterday? This doesn't mean that your life has to be perfect or saintly—only that you're faithfully growing as the Lord leads you.

In addition to being faithful to God and His Word,

faithfulness applies to your role as leader. Consider this commitment carefully before accepting. Do you have the time and interest to attend most of the meetings and to follow up with members? There's nothing more frustrating than a leader who doesn't show up, especially without making arrangements for someone else to cover the group. If you agree to lead, be faithful to that commitment. Make it a priority in your schedule. Commit both your schedule and your attitude to prayer, and strive to be an example of Christian faithfulness.

Read 2 Timothy 2:1-6. Like the faithful soldier, athlete, or farmer, we as leaders need to keep our eyes on the goal and our wills disciplined to the task before us. We need to present ourselves "to God as one approved, a workman who does not need to be ashamed and who correctly handles the word of truth" (2 Timothy 2:15).

However, there is another side to this commitment. Some leaders are *too* faithful! Leading your group is more important than your company's softball team or the latest soap on TV. The call to be faithful implies that you're willing to give up some of life's fleeting pleasures to give your time and energy to your group. But please, keep your group in its proper place—that is, below your responsibility to God, your spouse, and your children. Personally I think it's not only OK, but expected, for a leader to take off on his wife's or child's birthday. It's OK to take a family vacation and not return midweek for your group. It's OK to attend your daughter's graduation or your son's first Little League game. I've known leaders who are so compulsive about their "responsibility" that I question their priorities and judgment.

No one can give you a formula for setting your priorities as they relate to your group. But if your group routinely takes precedence over your relationship with God and your family, perhaps you need to reevaluate. If you need to make such decisions more than once a month, maybe it's not the time for you to be leading a group. Maybe you're not "available."

A Leader Must Be Available

In Ecclesiastes 3:1 King Solomon advises, "There is a time for everything, and a season for every activity under heaven." This wise admonition applies even to leading a Bible study. Some people are simply not in a season of their lives—or don't feel they are— where they can accept this responsibility. Consider your life-style, season in life, and priorities, then be honest about your availability. Seen this way, availability is an element of faithfulness.

For example, a person whose job requires a lot of travel may not be available for a weekly study. His life-style and priorities prevent such a commitment. Or a mother with three preschoolers may have a hard time keeping everyone healthy so she can be available as a leader. She may be in a season of life where she must limit her outside commitments.

On the other hand, if leading a study is God's priority for you, He will help you be available. It's easy to spot leaders who take their commitments seriously and those who don't.

When I was a leader in Careers, the singles ministry in San Francisco, it was truly my priority. Although I was an executive at a local hospital, I always left work in time for Bible study or meetings to which I had committed. I was simply unavailable for professional meetings on those nights. Later when I developed my own consulting practice, I continued to refuse business meetings that would conflict with my commitments to the group.

And God honored that commitment. It was never a problem. Bosses and clients alike respected my personal life. I don't remember it ever becoming an issue. During the years I was a consultant, my travel schedule was incredibly light, while others, who put their work first, were on the road more than half the time. Because of the priorities they had chosen, they were unavailable for ministry. Because ministry was my priority, God took care of my schedule.

However, now I'm in a different season. After years of leading various studies, I'm taking a break to write a series of Bible study guides. Now God has made it clear that He has other priorities for me—for this season, anyway.

Is serving as a leader one of your priorities? Is it God's priority for you? You won't be able to answer these questions in the excitement of the situation, but only in still, quiet prayer.

A Leader Must Be Teachable

Are you teachable? Are you willing to learn from others and from the Holy Spirit? Or are you puffed up with the pride of your superior knowledge or leadership skills? Can you learn, even from those you think know less than you? Remember that God uses the foolish things of the world to shame the wise—or those who think they're wise (1 Corinthians 1:26-31)! A good leader must be teachable.

A leader must be continually learning about the ways of God. This requires regular times of personal prayer and Bible study. It also requires an openness to the "still, small voice" of the Holy Spirit.

Being teachable requires that you put yourself in places where you can expand your knowledge of the Scriptures. The most obvious requirement is that every leader must be faithful in attending a solid, Bible-teaching church. Then take advantage of classes, seminars, and other learning opportunities in your area. Don't limit yourself to those within your own church or denomination. If you're well-grounded in the Word, you can greatly expand your understanding by exposing yourself to different perspectives. Keep an open mind, but don't be so open that your brains fall out. Always test what you hear against Scripture.

Not only do you need to learn about Scripture, but *you also need to grow in leadership skills.* Reading this book is a good start. When you finish it, read others. Again, gain several perspectives. I'll tell you everything I think is important about leading a small group Bible study, but I certainly can't exhaust the subject. And mine is only one opinion. There are many excellent books available for the teachable leader.

Are you taking advantage of leadership training sessions available in your church or ministry? What about training conducted by other ministries? Often instructors will allow you to sit in if they know you're serious. For example, the local leader of Nurses Christian Fellowship is a missionary supported by our church. When she conducted a leadership training session recently, she invited the leaders of our various women's Bible studies to attend. It was exciting to see both the similarities and the differences between our small groups.

Finally, *a good leader must be humble.* The subject of pride is touchy. We all know God's opinion of pride, yet who among us will readily confess to that sin? An attitude of pride or superiority can make the most knowledgeable Bible scholar useless. Unfortunately, it's often just such a person who covets and actively seeks leadership. That places a difficult burden on ministry leaders to maintain quality in their Bible studies.

If you want to be a leader, but are being passed over by those in charge, consider that you may have a bit of pride, manifesting itself in an unteachable spirit. Read and meditate on 1 Peter 5:5, 6.

"It is hard for a 'superior' person to be used of the Lord." —Richard C. Halverson

Maturity Where it Counts

∗

"Perseverance must finish its work so that you may be mature and complete, not lacking anything" (James 1:4).

A small group leader must also be mature. Now, that doesn't mean that you must have gray hair. Maturity is not only a function of age and tenure, but also of commitment. Scripture warns that we should not place a new convert in a position of leadership for his own protection and growth (1 Timothy 3:6). However, I know many who have matured so quickly that they could be trusted with a small group Bible study within a year or two of conversion, especially under the watchful eye of a more mature Christian. Sadly, there are also many who, after decades of being Christians, are still spiritual infants.

Does your life demonstrate a level of maturity that causes others to trust your judgment and leadership? Are you seeking to improve your walk with God each day? Are you an obedient Christian, or are there obvious or hidden sins with which you're not dealing?

Again, this doesn't mean that your life must be perfect. If perfection were a criterion for leadership, none of us would qualify! But are you confessing your faults daily? Are you diligently pursuing obedience? As the familiar saying goes, "Christians aren't perfect, they're just forgiven." Have you met the conditions for forgiveness?

A mature leader recognizes that life won't always follow the rose-strewn path. He knows that the more effective he is (or has the potential to be), the more evident will be the work of Satan in his life.

> "So far in the history of the world, there have never been enough mature people in the right places."
> —George B. Chisholm

One of the devil's greatest lies is that if you have any problems, you're disqualified from leadership. Some of the most effective leaders I've known have led in the midst of personal or family turmoil. But they qualified as leaders because they were open, vulnerable, and mature in the way they handled the stress. Instead of panicking, fretting, or whining about how tough life was, they simply remained open to the work of God in their lives. In the midst of learning lessons of faith in a difficult situation, they maintained their hope. And they shared the lessons they were learning with their group. There were no hidden skeletons, nor illusions of holiness or perfection. This attitude served as an object lesson for the group, increased openness among the members, and actually created respect for the leader.

A mature leader will know when to share the tough spots, when to share the warts, and when to be quiet. Don't you hate being around someone whose life is all honeysuckle and roses? I do, because it emphasizes how difficult my own life is. It's easy, then, to make unfair comparisons. It's tough to expect a "no-problem" leader to feel the sand in my shoe, so I tend to hobble along masking my own needs.

Of course, it's equally frustrating to be around a

person who is always struggling and seldom experiencing victory. Therefore, a mature leader will be sensitive to others and will know when and how to be appropriately vulnerable.

Leadership Through Servanthood

❋

"The greatest among you will be your servant" (Matthew 23:11).

They thought they had paid their dues. After all, they had followed the Master for almost three years. In fact, they were among His closest friends. And they did have certain administrative abilities not evident in some of the others. So James and John felt justified in asking for the honor of sitting on either side of Jesus when He came into His glory.

But Jesus set them straight. "You know that those who are regarded as rulers of the Gentiles lord it over them, and their high officials exercise authority over them. Not so with you. Instead, whoever wants to become great among you must be your servant, and whoever wants to be first must be slave of all." Then He continued, "For even the Son of Man did not come to be served, but to serve, and to give his life as a ransom for many" (Mark 10:42-45). A few days later He took the role of a servant, stooping to wash the filthy feet of each disciple.

"Wait a minute!" you say. "I signed on to be a leader, not a slave! You know, name in bright lights, everyone talking about what a good group we have, dozens on the waiting list!"

If that's your attitude, perhaps you need to reconsider. For the Christian, leadership operates from the bottom up. You lead by serving, by sacrificing, by giving of yourself. As a leader, you'll be expected to sacrifice your time, your energy, your effort, your resources, your very self. It's not an easy task. But it's a task that offers incredible rewards as you watch the members of your group grow toward maturity.

Once again, pride may try to creep in. Yet our example is Jesus, "who, being in the very nature God, did not consider equality with God something to be grasped, but made himself nothing, taking the very nature of a servant . . . he humbled himself and became obedient to death—even death on a cross!" (Philippians 2:6-8).

Few of us will literally give our lives for our groups. But we will have the opportunity to serve the members in a multitude of ways. We can expect frantic calls in the middle of the night. We may offer to baby-sit for a member's child when we'd rather not. We'll be asked to meet for additional prayer at inconvenient times. We may need to help another financially. Yet as we lovingly give of ourselves, the members of our group will move a step closer to maturity. And then, they will begin to serve others.

"The world is full of people who are standing on their dignity when they ought to be kneeling at the feet of their brethren."—William Barclay, *The Gospel of John, Volume 2*

As a leader, you'll seek the best, not only for each member of your group, but also for the whole group. Sometimes these goals will conflict with one another. We'll discuss how to handle this dilemma in Chapter 7, "Why Didn't You Warn Me?" Sometimes seeking the best for a group member will go against your own self-interest. How will you handle that?

Rooted in Prayer

✻

"The prayer of a righteous man is powerful and effective" (James 5:16).

Do you believe in prayer? Do you pray? Sometimes the answers to those two questions are very different. I'm sure that anyone reading this book can answer an enthusiastic "Yes!" to the first question. But what of the second?

Do you pray? Do you pray daily, fervently, believing God for the answers? When you pray, do you touch the mind and heart of God? Is prayer a priority in your life?

Even more revealing is the question, "What don't you pray for?" The Lord jarred me with that question while writing a Bible study chapter on prayer. I realized there are several needs for which I no longer pray. And the reasons were most convicting! What do *you* no longer pray for? Why?

As a leader, I must be a pray-er. I must realize that

leading a small group Bible study is a spiritual endeavor. Regardless of my personal leadership skills, if the Lord does not build this group, I'm wasting my time. I need His wisdom and His guidance or we'll simply have a nice visit each week.

What should you pray for? Pray for your group members and their individual needs. Pray for the group as a whole.

When a member shares a concern with you, do you pray right then and there? Out loud with the person if that's appropriate? And do you continue to remember the person in prayer throughout the week? I've found that often, when a group seems not to be jelling well, it's because I haven't been praying for the members and they haven't been praying for one another.

"The tragedy of our day is not unanswered prayer, but unoffered prayer." —Ruth Bell Graham

How will you know? When you meet, who remembers last week's prayer requests? Chances are, those who don't remember from week to week haven't been praying. As the leader, are you setting the example?

As members of your group begin to grow, to reach toward maturity, you can expect them to face enemy warfare (read Ephesians 6:10-18; 1 Peter 5:8, 9). Pray constantly for them so God may count them worthy of His calling. Pray that, by His power, He may fulfill every good purpose in them. Pray that their lives will glorify the name of the Lord Jesus (2 Thessalonians 1:11, 12).

The Leader as a Model

✳

"Set an example for the believers in speech, in life, in love, in faith, and in purity" (1 Timothy 4:12).

When I was a child, one of my father's favorite sayings was, "Do as I say, not as I do!" This warning came when one of us children caught him violating his own rules. I wonder if some of that attitude doesn't permeate the church today.

The apostle Paul, speaking to the Corinthian church, was bold enough to say, "Follow my example, as I follow the example of Christ" (1 Corinthians 11:1). Can you say that? Can you encourage your group members to follow your example as you follow Christ? Are you an example for others in every aspect of your life? Or might you find yourself saying, "Do as I say, not as I do?"

How will your group members learn openness and vulnerability? From watching you, their leader, be open and vulnerable. How will they learn how to be accountable to one another? By watching you hold yourself accountable to them. How will they learn the importance of the Scriptures in developing a godly life? From watching how important God's Word is to you. How will they learn servanthood? By watching you serve them.

Being a model is an awesome responsibility. Yet the church today needs men and women others can follow with confidence. Are you willing to be a model for those who trust you as leader?

> "People seldom improve when they have no model but themselves to copy after."
> —Oliver Goldsmith

Another arena where we need unselfish models is that of sharing leadership itself. During my residency in hospital administration, my preceptor often challenged, "Pat, you can consider yourself a success when you've worked yourself out of a job." That lesson has served me well, both in my professional life and in my role as a leader. Set as your goal always to model, encourage, and share leadership. Then you can be free to move on to other areas where God calls you. And let's face it—a good leader is always in demand. If you work yourself out of a job here, a dozen other opportunities will clamor for your attention!

When I knew I needed to leave the Moms' Bible Study to complete this series, I felt not only personal sadness, but also some reluctance. I had planned to devote three years to preparing the leadership team to take over, with the third year being the one where I would fade into the background. But God had other plans. It was clear I was to leave after only two years.

After a couple of leadership meetings, I was able to leave without concern. Since the entire leadership team had worked closely together from the beginning, there were several women capable of taking over the ministry without ever missing a beat. And as they've added their own personal touches, the ministry has improved and is serving even more women than before.

It's human nature to want to be indispensible. It boosted my ego to feel that the group would fall apart without me. But God calls each of us to model leadership, train up new leaders, and be willing to move on at the right time. That's called discipleship.

Paul planted a lot of churches. But he would only stay in any one place until he had trained and stabilized the leadership. Then he moved on. Likewise, Barnabas, Silas, and Timothy trained others and moved on. Think how much slower the spread of Christianity would have been if Paul had felt that he was the only one capable of leading each church he planted!

And really, isn't it the height of insult to keep your group dependent on you? Like a parent whose goal is to release free mature adults, a leader's goal should be to develop groups that can function, sustain themselves, and even grow for years after we've moved on.

Exhibiting Spiritual Fruit

✳

"But the fruit of the Spirit is love, joy, peace, patience, kindness, goodness, faithfulness, gentleness and self-control" (Galatians 5:22, 23).

Jesus warned the Pharisees, perhaps the most "qualified" leaders of His day, that "a tree is recognized by its fruit" (Matthew 12:33). As leaders we're known by our fruit, whether good or bad.

The apostle Paul contrasted the fruit of the sinful nature with the fruit of the Spirit in Galatians 5:19-23. Take time now to read Galatians 5:13-26. Consider how the fruit of the flesh or sinful nature should disqualify any Christian from leadership.

But what of the fruit of the Spirit? Paul says that if we're living by the Spirit, we'll exhibit love, joy, peace, patience, kindness, goodness, faithfulness, gentleness, and self-control. That's a tall order for most of us! It's also a process of growth.

The most important truth to remember about this fruit is that it's just that—fruit. It develops, not from our own straining, striving efforts, but from simply abiding in Christ. Jesus said, "I am the vine; you are the branches. If a man remains in me and I in him, he will bear much fruit; apart from me you can do nothing" (John 15:5).

If you're having a hard time identifying this fruit in your life, perhaps you're trying to live life apart from the Vine. Give more time and more of yourself to abiding and clinging to the living Lord. Seek the transforming presence of the Holy Spirit and rest in Him. Then you'll see a remarkable increase in the fruit of the Spirit and a remarkable decrease in the fruit of the flesh. And you'll become an increasingly effective leader.

"Notice that this is the fruit of the Spirit. It is not our fruit. The Holy Spirit is the One who lives the life of Christ in us. We don't live it ourselves. Instead, we live in it. *The fruit of the Spirit is the character and life of Jesus Christ being lived out of us by the Holy Spirit.* We don't get this character from God; we get God Who is this character. This is God's very own life coming to live in us through the Holy Spirit"*

*Richard Booker, *Seated in Heavenly Places*. South Plainfield, NJ: Bridge Publishing. Copyright © 1986.

CHAPTER 3

Keys to Changed Lives

IN CHAPTER 1 we discussed some assumptions about the type of small group, or the structure of a group that leads to maximum spiritual growth and maturity. In Chapter 2 we examined seven qualities that are important to any leader. Now we need to examine seven elements of a small group that are essential to effectively change lives and bring participants to maturity. These seven elements include nurture, worship, mission, community, transparency, accountability, and prayer. The best groups will incorporate all seven elements. Let's look at each individually.

"They devoted themselves to the apostles' teaching and to the fellowship, to the breaking of bread and to prayer" (Acts 2:42).

Nurture

❋

"Jesus said, 'Feed my sheep'" (John 21:17).

This book assumes you will use a published study guide or perhaps one written by someone else and provided to you. If you're leading without a study guide, or if you're writing your own questions as you go along, you'll need to adapt this information to suit your situation.

The element of nurture relates to the ability of your group to provide spiritual food or nourishment for each member. The nurture of the group will come largely from the quality and the appropriateness of the Bible study guide you select. This may be one of the most important decisions that you as a leader will make.

There are hundreds of studies on the market. Won't just any of them do? No! An emphatic no! The next chapter discusses the specific elements to look for in a sound Bible study. In this chapter we'll consider finding the right study for your group.

I'm amazed at how many people overlook the basics here. A good study for your group must be pertinent. It must contribute to each person's growth. That implies something, doesn't it? The leader must know something about his group and choose an appropriate study for them.

As a leader you must know your group's real and felt needs. What are those? A person's felt needs are those he or she can identify readily. The individual feels the need and can almost always name it. A person's real needs are deeper and are often a mystery. He or she may not be able to tell you what they are until they've been met. They often relate to the person's motivations or the roots underlying the felt needs.

For example, my husband participated in a group that ministered to Christian dads. The felt needs of these men were to be better fathers in a complex world. The felt needs drew them together as a group. Many of the topics of discussion addressed their felt needs.

The men's real needs, however, may have been different. One, a new Christian, struggled with integrating his new-found faith into his daily roles as husband, father, friend, and employee. An executive knew that his next promotion would demand more travel, but felt trapped by the corporate ladder he's

chosen to climb. Another seldom had time for Bible
study and prayer. He knew he was running on empty,
but couldn't begin to figure out a solution. Another
with a wayward child needed affirmation and encouragement. A leader who understands this will select a
study that not only addresses the felt needs, but also
can penetrate to minister to at least some of the underlying or real needs.

List everything
you know about
your group.
Then use that
checklist as you
select your study
guide.

Do you know where your group members are likely
to be hurting? Do you know how mature they are as
Christians? Do you know how they live and what
issues excite them?

Does that mean that your group needs to meet first
so you can get to know everyone's real needs, then
choose the study? Not necessarily. You may know
many of the members through your church, singles
group, or job. Or, lacking that, you probably know a
bit about the type of people you'll have in your group.
This is one place where having a group of similar
people is helpful.

When I started the Moms' Bible Study, I knew only
a few other moms personally. However, I knew
enough to make some generalizations about this group
of women. For example, I knew that few of us were
acquainted with many of the other moms; our church
provided no opportunities for that to happen. I knew
that most of the women who were home during the
day were mothers of preschoolers, and most were in
their 20's; a few were in their 30's and 40's. I knew
the moms' primary interests were in becoming better
mothers, in building stronger marriages, and in coping
with the stress of living on one income in an expensive
area. And finally, I knew many of the moms had not
developed strong study habits, and some were fairly
new Christians.

"The choice of
what to study
should be made
with the
backgrounds
and interests of
the group
members in
mind." —Roberta
Hestenes, *Using
the Bible in
Groups*

With these knowns in mind the other leaders and I
were able to select studies that met many of their
needs, providing them with a firm foundation for their
faith and for the various roles they filled. We were also
able to tailor the discussions to pinpoint even more
specifically the primary issues in their lives.

The key in selecting any study guide, then, is to identify a biblically sound study that addresses both the felt and the real needs of the group that will use it.

Worship

✳

"Come, let us bow down in worship, let us kneel before the Lord our Maker" (Psalm 95:6).

It seems obvious that a small group dedicated to Christian growth and Bible study would include worship. However, I'm amazed at how few groups actually incorporate this essential element as more than a superficial exercise.

In worship, we ascribe worth to God. We acknowledge who He is. We affirm His character. We praise Him for who He is rather than for what He's done for us.

Worship can take many forms. It need not be limited to singing, but can also include the reading of psalms, prayers, devotional thoughts, or many other writings. It can incorporate silent meditation or cheers and clapping. It may even feature dance, pantomime, or drama.

There are many reasons for overlooking worship. Some people have not experienced true worship and therefore don't miss it. Others know it's important but feel that they just don't have time in their tight group schedule to include it. Still others, who equate worship with singing, beg off, insisting that they can't carry a tune in a bucket.

As legitimate as these reasons—or any others—may appear, they simply aren't valid. There is no excuse for neglecting worship in a small group Bible study. Bible study is not an academic activity. It's a spiritual endeavor, and to see lives changed, we need to experience the presence of God.

You may reason that simply opening in prayer will call the Holy Spirit into the midst of the group; that should be adequate. You're right, of course. We don't need to jump through the hoop of worship to persuade God to be present among us. He has promised that "where two or three come together in my name, there am I with them" (Matthew 18:20). But, we also know that God inhabits the praises of His people (Psalm 22:3). Worship pleases God. He lives in, dwells in, makes himself at home in the midst of our praise. What better reason for spending time worshiping Him?

However, worship does more than please God. It also serves an important purpose for us. If our goal is to encourage the spiritual growth of each person in our group, we need to begin our time together by entering into God's presence—not simply by asking Him to enter into our presence.

Let's face it. It doesn't matter whether your study is on Sunday morning, during lunch on Wednesday, or after dinner on Friday, people are going to rush to get there on time. That's just the nature of our lives these days. We all have too much to do in too little time. Murphy's law is resident with each of us. So we rush into the study a bit winded, with at least a dozen demands and frustrations competing for our attention. Our thoughts and unfinished tasks pull us in every direction, while Satan does his part to prevent us from enjoying quality time with our Lord.

That's why we need to start with worship. We need to open ourselves to the calming presence of Holy Spirit. We need to experience awe as we enter the presence of the King of Kings and Lord of Lords. We need to sit at the feet of Jesus and listen to His voice. Most of us simply can't do that with an opening prayer. We can't change gears that fast. We need help in making the transition from the world to the Word.

So whatever you neglect, please don't neglect opening with a time of worship.

Guidelines for Worship

For some of us, beginning a group meeting with worship is as natural as getting up in the morning. For others it's a frightening, unknown mine field. This is especially true if your church's tradition is not one of active participation and freedom in worship.

I can't tell you there is one way to worship. What I'm comfortable with may not work for you and your

"The measure of the worth of our public activity for God is the private profound communion we have with Him. Rush is wrong every time, there is always plenty of time to worship God."
—Oswald Chambers, *My Utmost for His Highest*

group. But I'd suggest that most of us have a limited concept of worship. We prefer either the formal or the informal and often look with disdain on the other side. I want to encourage you to use your time together to explore various forms of worship. Set a goal of growing in this area of your Christian life.

It's not the purpose of this book to be an exhaustive manual on worship, but let's look at a few guidelines to make your time of praise more effective and rewarding.

Allow enough time for worship. Many groups simply open with a couple of songs. While that is an improvement over no worship at all, realize that it takes time for most people to enter the presence of the Lord. Allow at least ten minutes for your worship time—twice that if you possibly can. I know that the more limited your time together is the more difficult it will be to give up much time for worship. But try it. You'll find that the Lord will somehow restore to you the time spent in worship.

Be sure that worship is participative. In your limited time together members should actively participate in most, if not all, of the worship exercises. Occasionally a solo or reading may be appropriate, but most of us need to do more than listen to enter the presence of God.

Many people find it helpful to stand during worship, especially for singing. Not only is it easier to sing while standing, but a change of position also helps keep the attention from wandering and keeps the blood circulating.

For the same reason, it's also helpful to develop a repertoire of songs people can sing from memory. It's easier to enter the presence of God when you can close your eyes and concentrate on Him. We've suggested some worship resources in Appendix A.

These guidelines will be most difficult to implement if your group meets in a public place like a restaurant, park, or office. If you can't comfortably sing, consider a reading or devotional with some discussion to make it participative.

"Ascribe to the Lord the glory due his name; worship the Lord in the splendor of his holiness" (Psalm 29:2).

Allow worship to flow without human interruption.
This is difficult but essential. The most effective worship allows the Holy Spirit uninterrupted access to the
deepest parts of our hearts and minds. In prayer, meditation and worship we enter the dimension of God that
is beyond the level of our well-controlled conscious-
ness. Each time the leader interrupts that flow to
announce another song or to editorialize, it draws the
worshiper back to the alert level and hinders the work
God is doing. The more that worship can flow without
interruption, the more effective it will be in drawing
the group members into the presence of Almighty
God. This doesn't mean that the worship leader can't
speak at all. Sometimes a well thought out, prayerful
comment can smooth a transition and, in fact, enhance
the worship experience. We've all seen this done
effectively. However, it's a skill that is learned and
developed over time. It comes naturally to very few.

"It is only when
men begin to
worship that
they begin to
grow." —Calvin
Coolidge

Don't shy away from special music, Bible reading,
devotional reading, or verbal prayer. Variety is essential to avoid monotony, but integrate that variety into
the tone and pace of the worship. This might mean, for
example, that you don't introduce a soloist before he
sings or applaud when he's finished. Rather, allow the
solo to blend inconspicuously and appropriately into
the worship time. The group can continue quietly worshiping with silent meditation or words of praise following the song. The key is to consider such specials
as an integral part of worship, not as a performance.

Try something new once in a while. If your group is
traditional and prefers hymns, occasionally add a praise
chorus or two. If they thrive on choruses, introduce
some of the great hymns of the faith. If it's not your
tradition to raise your hands in praise, try it with an
appropriate song. Suggest standing, kneeling, or clapping hands at times.

Often when we worship the same way week after
week, the time becomes predictable, stale, and ineffec-
tive. You want to broaden your group members' experiences. Occasionally move them just beyond their comfort zone so God can work in a new way. You don't

want to go too far too fast, and you'll want to keep most of their experiences comfortable. But both formal and informal worship have much to commend them.

As you try different forms of worship, talk about them. For some reason talking about worship is uncomfortable for many people. It's almost as if it's too personal, too private to share. I don't believe this attitude pleases God any more than if we *only* talk about it. Seek to gain a common understanding of worship within your group.

Search the Scriptures for new insights on worship. Begin in the Psalms. Proceed to Isaiah, Hebrews, and Revelation. The more you learn about who God is and how others have worshiped Him throughout history, the more you'll long to experience the presence of the living God and to share that experience with your group. Who can read Psalm 8, Isaiah 6, Hebrews 4, or Revelation 4 and 5 without crying out in praise and adoration to our God?

As you seek examples of worship in God's Word, you'll gain a marvelous new freedom in this vital aspect of Christian life.

The Healing Ministry of Worship

If some members of your group need spiritual, emotional, or even physical healing, they may gain far more from deep, extended periods of worship than from all the studies you can give them. Worship is probably the most therapeutic activity a Christian can engage in. This is particularly true for those who are good students and can easily turn a Bible study into a quest for more knowledge. Allow the Spirit of the living God to move deeply among your group. They will never be the same again.

"The Lord gives strength to his people; the Lord blesses his people with peace" (Psalm 29:11).

You may find that those who need it the most criticize the time devoted to worship. They have better things to do. A particularly depressed person may complain, "I just can't get into it." My response for such a person is, "Be faithful. Keep trying. Persevere. It may take years, but God will honor your faithfulness, and your relationship with Him will never be the same again."

I can attest to this. Several years ago a combination of life's darts had rendered me almost useless. I saw no point in going on. I questioned if God was really even there. I was severely depressed. When my own church could offer no relief I began attending the evening prayer and praise service at another local church. This service offers an extended time of worship, testimony, and prayer, with very little teaching. At first I just sat there. I couldn't understand how all those people were so caught up in worship. But I was faithful. I kept showing up because I knew I needed to.

Over a three-year period I grew to the point where now I can truly worship my Lord anywhere. And in the process I've been healed, not instantaneously, but gently, slowly, uniquely, and deeply by the Lord I worship.

I still firmly believe in Bible study. It's still my desire to see each Christian gain a firm understanding of the Word of God. But now I know that this can't be done without the Spirit of God, whom we touch when we worship.

If your group feels a little flat, begin to worship. It will take time—maybe even years for some people— but worship will break down strongholds that nothing else will penetrate.

> "Worship renews the spirit as sleep renews the body."
> —Richard Clarke Cabot

I thought this was a Bible study! Now we have a mission?

Each group has a mission. It's just that most don't talk about it, so no one is clear on what it is. This is one reason why many groups flounder after awhile. Your mission is your group's reason for existing. It answers the question, "Why is this particular group together at this particular time and place?" And it's not as easy to answer as you might think.

"We're here to do Bible study, of course," you answer. OK. But what kind of Bible study? This gets

Mission

❋

> "May the God who gives endurance and encouragement give you a spirit of unity among yourselves as you follow Christ Jesus" (Romans 15:5)

back to the group's original purpose for being together. Just what is it that you want to get out of the Bible?

Let's look at an example. You crave spiritual growth. In fact, you want a radical discipleship group that will help conform more and more areas of your life to the lordship of Jesus Christ. Most people in your group don't even know what that means. One man is a fairly new Christian still grappling with the basics. An older woman is going through a divorce and wants a quick fix. Two young moms need fellowship and a night out. Their husbands came primarily at their wives' insistence. Although they know the importance of Bible study, they don't have a lot of time or energy to commit to it.

"More men fail through lack of purpose than through lack of talent."—Billy Sunday

I can almost guarantee that your group will never jell. There are simply too many different reasons for being there. The study will limp along with each person seeking and giving what he or she can, but never feeling satisfied. This group will frustrate you. Soon you'll wonder why you ever thought you could lead a Bible study.

Most of this frustration can be avoided if you take a few precautionary steps in the beginning.

Finding Common Ground

There are as many ways to define your group's mission as there are ways groups get started. As the leader, you need to take the initiative.

If you haven't formed your group yet, the easiest way to do this is to determine what you believe God wants, then seek like-minded members. While this is the most effective way to form a group, it may also be difficult. For example, for several years I've been looking for people interested in a serious discipleship group. They're rare—and the few of us interested haven't been able to find a common time when we can meet.

A friend and I began with the selective approach when we developed a "How to Be Happy Though Single" group for the singles ministry in San Francisco.

We defined the purpose, content, format, and length of time the group would meet. Then we invited people individually, being very clear so they knew what they were agreeing to. In 14 years of leading or participating in groups, I've never been part of a more dynamic, cohesive, committed group than that one was. A common, pre-defined mission bound us together.

But even building a group around your vision can backfire unless you're specific in defining the mission of the group, and exclusive about who you allow to join. When we started the Moms' Bible Study, which was open to all moms in the church, the leaders knew our primary goal. We wanted a mechanism to meet the moms' needs for consistent Bible study. The studies we selected addressed these needs. However, our first evaluation yielded a surprise. Although the women recognized their need for Bible study, what they valued most was the fellowship with other moms. We needed to modify the original schedule and the format to better meet their needs. In effect, we changed the mission.

"Vision does not come by inspiration. It comes from knowledge, intelligently cultivated."
—Robert A. Weaver

At the first meeting, I always try to articulate what I see as the mission for the group and to encourage discussion of others' views. If the group will continue for more than about 12 weeks, it's a good idea to check its pulse periodically and make sure that the mission hasn't changed. Even if it hasn't changed, it's a good idea to affirm the mission once a month or so. This helps remind each member why they joined the group and where they're heading. You are, in fact, the keeper of the vision.

Many groups like to formalize their mission by signing an agreement or group covenant. In the covenant you can spell out the mission of the group, as well as agreements on other responsibilities such as attendance, participation, homework, relationships, and membership. The process of negotiating the covenant allows everyone to have a voice in the development of the group and allows no one the excuse of "I didn't know. . . ." A sample group covenant is presented in Appendix B.

The Scope of Mission

The mission of your group may be internal, external, or both. It may be broad, narrow, or both. It's important to define your purpose up front, although the emphasis may shift over time.

A group with an internal mission focuses primarily on the growth of its members. The study selected emphasizes this mission. Prayer time focuses almost exclusively on members' needs. The group takes on few, if any, outside ministries as a group. The mission is broad, allowing people to take what they need and give what they can. The Moms' Bible Study is internal and broad. It meets a wide spectrum of needs with little conflict through various activities.

Even in such a group there is ministry. It's just that the ministries are individual. I lead a Bible study, you teach Sunday school, and she works in a Crisis Pregnancy Center. We each have a ministry, but the only time the group interfaces with that ministry is when we ask them to pray for a specific need. Since these ministries are scattered, the mission is internal and broad.

A group with an external mission is one that focuses on something or someone outside of the group. For example, as a group you may support a missionary, pray for revival in the nation, or engage in social activism. Your Bible study will probably relate closely to the mission. Your ministries are "focused," so your mission is external and narrowly defined.

Of course, broad doesn't always go with internal, and narrow with external. Our church's substance abuse group is internal (focusing on the needs of the group members and their families) and narrow (dealing specifically with the impact of the substance abuse on those lives). Ted's evangelistic Bible study is external (reaching out to others) and broad (meeting a wide spectrum of needs).

You can see how important it is to define mission up front. If I'm expecting a focused social action group and you want a Bible study that stresses spiritual depth, we may or may not be able to find a

"It is important for all Christian small groups to give some consideration to ministry, for the gospel life essentially runs on two tracks, the journey inward and the journey outward. Each of these tracks supports the other. To do the work of God, we must be the people of God. Conversely, engaging in mission strengthens the bonds of fellowship and provides a needed dimension to our experience as community."
—Bob Parker, *Small Groups: Workable Wineskins*

common ground. Should we form a group? That depends on how much common ground we can find.

The Consequences of No Mission

What happens if you have a group with a poorly defined mission, or one that everyone hasn't understood or agreed to? You'll find that members will opt out of, or choose not to participate in, those parts of the group they haven't specifically agreed to. And chances are, that will cause hurt feelings, anger, or bitterness. It will erode the sense of community in the group. It's a problem you'll want to avoid.

There are many examples of such a situation. Linda joined the Bible study to study the Bible. She doesn't have time for fellowship—she has plenty of that elsewhere. The women in the group decide to go out for dinner together. Linda stays home, pleading that she's too busy. She misses out on this bonding time and doesn't fit in as well after that.

Jim is committed to the pro-life movement. He spends his weekends participating in Operation Rescue or picketing abortion clinics. He can't understand why everyone doesn't do this, so he spends his time at Bible study berating the other members for not joining him. Soon several others stop coming. They joined a Bible study, not a social action group.

Both of these situations become even more complicated if either Linda or Jim is the group leader. But of course, *you* would never let that happen. Take the time in the beginning to define your group's mission and you'll find it to be time well spent.

"All Christian small groups should develop a clear sense of purpose. The group members should all understand this purpose and promise to work toward achieving it." —Roberta Hestenes, *Using the Bible in Groups*

Community

"They broke bread in their homes and ate together with glad and sincere hearts, praising God and enjoying the favor of all the people" (Acts 2:46, 47)

For many groups, community is the primary reason for the group's existence.

Closely related to mission is the sphere of community or fellowship. Community in a small group Bible study relates to the sense of "connectedness" members of the group have with one another. It focuses on knowing others and being known by them.

Many people today, especially those under 40, join groups more for relationships than for Bible study. Our lives are hurried and fragmented. We long for that sense of community that was natural with our pioneer forefathers 100 years ago. We need to belong. We need to know and to be known. We need community.

This used to bother me. After all, God had called me to lead a Bible study, not a coffee klatch. I'd get frustrated with groups in which people weren't as anxious as I to "get down to business."

It took a while for me to realize that fellowship is "business." It's God's business, just as Bible study is God's business. We don't worship a one-dimensional God; He doesn't want us to be one-dimensional people. He cares about every aspect of our lives. He cares about our spiritual growth, but He also cares about our emotional needs.

Since this is true, we must design our groups so we offer the members what they want, while also offering them the healing balm of a good Bible study, good worship, and a clear mission. The key is balance. We must strive for a balance in all that we do in our groups. A group that is all Bible study with no sense of community won't cause deep changes in lives. But chances are a group formed solely for fellowship won't either. We need to develop a balance between fellowship and study, sharing and prayer, social times and study times. Then we will have a true community.

"In our churches we speak so often of 'community' as though it were something relatively easy to achieve. However such is not the case. We seek to build 'Christian community' through fellowships and socials, and although these may have helped build some relationships, these do not get at the basic matter of community. . . . Community is a *quality* of relationships. The number of people with whom we can be related casually in a particular grouping can be quite large. However, the number of people with whom we can be 'in community' is necessarily small. It is a relationship in which I can come to be known and be known in depth."*

*Findley B. Edge, in the introduction to William Clemmons and Harvey Hester, *Growth Through Groups*

How Do We Get There?

We've defined community as knowing others and being known by them, or as fellowship. We've suggested that it's as essential in developing a good group as is the quality of the study. So how do we get there? How do we maintain the proper balance?

Starting with a like-minded group of people is helpful. We've talked about this in previous sections. If people have several common elements in their lives community will develop more quickly than if they are all different.

If the members of your group don't know one another or have little in common you can help them connect by structuring the early meetings to enhance fellowship. Give people the opportunity to share from several aspects of their lives in your opening exercises. The more aspects they share, the more likely group members are to find common ground.

Even after the first meeting, plan some time for fellowship within each meeting. If you don't plan it, people will take it anyway—and probably at times you'd rather they wouldn't! Depending on when and for how long you meet, your options are many. Have the coffee or tea ready 15 minutes before the starting time. Early arrivals can gather around the coffee pot and visit. Announce this as a time for fellowship, but be faithful to starting the group on time.

People can also linger after the study. Especially in an evening study I like to serve refreshments at the

"So true fellowship is more than eating apple pie together, although that is a part of it. Essentially it is sharing life together in a loving, caring manner. It is that part of group life where we minister to one another in a variety of situations, from 'weeping with those who weep to rejoicing with those who rejoice' (Romans 12:15)." —Bob Parker, *Small Groups: Workable Wineskins*

end, allowing almost unlimited time for people to connect, but also freeing people to escape if they need to.

In addition to "in group" time, you'll want some extended times for people to get to know one another. Plan a dinner at a restaurant, a pot luck, or a social outing early in the life of your group and repeat as necessary to develop true community. Be sure that social times maximize interaction. Simply going to a movie together won't do a lot for community; a picnic, ski trip, or hike will. As your group jells, you'll find that growth occurs through community in places or ways that it doesn't in Bible study.

Create Ownership in the Group

Creating ownership in the group is related to community. This is a lesson I learned the hard way. You can learn from my error.

When we started the Moms' Bible Study, I was an experienced leader. I thought I knew what I was doing. The church where we met had a large room that we used for our gathering time. The other leaders and I set it up theater style, with a podium at the front from which I could make introductory announcements.

We began the first meeting having taken care of each detail. Everything was perfect. Since the first meeting typically doesn't have a lot of interaction, we didn't think much about how quiet the group was. But as time went on we found that we couldn't get the members to comment on or volunteer for anything. I felt as if I were talking to a blank wall! It was awful! Week after week the women just stared at me.

After several weeks I realized my mistake. I had given the impression that this was my group. I hadn't created ownership among the women in the group. I don't remember ever consciously doing this before, but with this group it was essential. What could I do?

One morning I expressed my concern over their lack of involvement. I assured them that I had no intention of having the study revolve around me. They needed to own the group, to care about it, to pray for

"[Ownership is] when each person feels a personal stake in the success or failure of the group. . . . When I make the group's aim my own personal goal, I'm tied in with something bigger than myself." —Em Griffin, *Getting Together*

it, to make it their own. I reminded them that they would never gain much from the Bible study until the group began to look more like them and less like me. And I expressed my willingness to even dissolve the group if they didn't care enough to own it.

The change was remarkable. That very morning a few women ventured opinions. Another volunteered for a task that needed to be done. The next week a few more took responsibility and rearranged the room while the leaders were in another area praying.

The room arrangement proved to be a key in creating ownership in this group. The women moved several tables into the center of the room so we could sit in a large circle looking at one another. That helped a lot. I started making announcements sitting at the table with the rest of the women. That made me more a part of the group. Gone was the feeling that I was the big leader who was going to do everything my way. Although I don't think my words had given that impression, the room arrangement was too similar to the sanctuary where the attention is focused on the minister and where there's little interaction among the congregation.

We discuss space considerations in further detail in Chapter 5.

After these changes the women truly owned the group. And because I had diminished as a focal point, I was able, a couple of years later, to take a leave of absence without creating a big void. Had I continued to own the group and have it revolve around me, one of two things would have happened. Either it would have dissolved from lack of interest or it would have become so dependent on me that it couldn't continue without me. As you consider your room arrangement do your best to create a sense of equality among all members, including yourself. In a home you won't have much of a choice, but in a church building you probably have some latitude. Make your decisions based on the goal of creating ownership within the group.

Trans-parency

✳

"We are not like Moses, who would put a veil over his face to keep the Israelites from gazing at it while the radiance was fading away" (2 Corinthians 3:13)

"The only basis for real fellowship with God and man is to live out in the open with both."—Roy Hession

Closely related to community is transparency, or honesty. If people hope to grow toward maturity within the group, each person needs to be honest and transparent with the others.

This is tough and it takes time to develop in most groups. We all wear veils, just as Moses wore a veil on his face to hide the fading glory of the Lord (2 Corinthians 3:13). We hide the deep truths about ourselves from one another, fearing rejection or criticism. We wonder what others would think if they really knew us.

Yet growth seldom occurs in isolation. It's too easy to deceive ourselves. It's too easy to justify, rationalize, or downplay the very areas that the Holy Spirit wants to open to the light. Jesus said, "This is the verdict: Light has come into the world, but men loved darkness instead of light because their deeds were evil. Everyone who does evil hates the light, and will not come into the light for fear that his deeds will be exposed. But whoever lives by the truth comes into the light, so that it may be seen plainly that what he has done has been done through God" (John 3:19-21). We need one another to shine the light of truth on those areas we'd as soon keep hidden. But others in our group can only do that when we are honest and transparent with them. And that's not easy.

This is the main reason I recommend against most mixed groups unless the mission of the group is to improve the members' marriages. Otherwise it's just too difficult to disclose our faults or needs when our husband or wife—or someone else's husband or wife —is listening. This is especially true if, as is so common today, the husband and wife aren't already communicating and praying together privately. In mixed singles groups, romantic desires or fear can easily inhibit transparency.

Nurturing Transparency

If honest disclosure and transparency are so difficult to achieve, is there any hope? How can you and I, as leaders of small groups, ever hope to love people to the point where they will allow the Holy Spirit to illumine the tender areas?

It's not easy, but it begins with you as the leader. You must set both the pace and the tone. Setting the pace means that the more deeply and honestly *you* share, the more deeply and honestly your group will share. Setting the tone incorporates three guidelines that are of utmost importance in nurturing honesty within your group. These three are empathy, warmth, and respect, which Dr. Gary Sweeten calls the "core conditions" of a helping relationship.*

Setting the pace. No one expects you to be perfect. When you the leader verbalize your weaknesses and needs honestly, it gives others "permission" to begin slowly, carefully, tentatively to open themselves to the group and to the Holy Spirit.

That means you must be willing to take a risk. You must be vulnerable and share at a level that the others won't match immediately. It also means that you won't want to dive to the deepest pit in the first meeting. You'll scare everyone off! But as you peel away your veils like the layers on an onion, and if you have also set the tone to make honest disclosure safe, you can expect those in your group to begin doing the same.

Setting the tone—empathy. Empathy communicates understanding of the other person's needs, feelings, or ideas. As the leader you need to model empathy for the other members of your group, and if necessary, teach them how to communicate with empathy.

Empathy does not say, "I know exactly how you feel." Even if we've experienced the same event, it's been screened through a different grid of emotions, personal history, and coping mechanisms. Rather, empathy says, "I understand what the issue is, and I

"Lord, who may dwell in your sanctuary? . . . He whose walk is blameless and who does what is righteous, who speaks the truth from his heart." (Psalm 15:1, 2)

*The information included in this section is based on *Apples of Gold: Developing the Fruit of the Spirit for Life and Ministry* by Dr. Gary Sweeten: copyright © 1981 by Christian Information Committee, Inc., Cincinnati, OH

understand how you're feeling about it." An empathic response communicates an *accurate* perception of both the *content* of the issue and the speaker's *feelings* about that issue.

A strongly empathic response might be, "It sounds as if you are feeling very angry because your boss passed you over for the promotion." The content is what happened—you were passed over for the promotion. The feelings are the person's response to the event—anger.

A response that does not show empathy may have one of several characteristics. These are based on an empathy rating scale developed by Robert Carkhuff.* If you see any of these in your group you need to intercept them quickly and show your group members a better way:

*This information is from *Helping and Human Relations,* Volumes 1 and 2 by Robert R. Carkhuff, copyright © 1969. Published by Holt, Rinehart, and Winston.

Attack or hurt the sharer, making him wish he'd never spoken. "You shouldn't be upset about the promotion. You couldn't handle any more work anyway!"

Miss the surface feelings and content. This response doesn't attack, but it's irrelevant. It's often a "fix-it" response. Such a reaction might be, "Well, maybe you should just go and get a new job."

Only partially respond to surface feelings, but have an accurate perception of the content. This response is often a "bumper sticker" response—a quick, catchy slogan. "Well, you know that all things work together for good. You'll probably get a better promotion!"

Only partially respond to content, but have an accurate perception of the feeling. This response borders on an attack. "Boy are you upset! You know, anger never wins; it just gives ulcers."

Setting the tone—warmth. Warmth focuses on nonverbal communication, which researchers say makes up 55 to 65 percent or more of all communication. This includes body movement, voice quality, and environmental surroundings. We send nonverbal signals all the time. It's important to learn to identify them in those talking and those listening. As leaders, it's important to model warmth in all we do.

Nonverbal signals sent by various parts of our bodies often communicate our feelings or attitudes louder than our words. The head, face, mouth, shoulders, arms, and legs, as well as the total body itself, provide valuable information about how a person is feeling. A person who is uncomfortable may cross his arms or legs, as if to create a barrier between himself and the rest of the group. He may look away, avoiding eye contact. Learn to read these signals to gain a deeper understanding of the person's feelings about what he's saying.

As you listen to a member's sharing, maintain an open body yourself. That is, don't cross your arms or legs, which communicate distance or a barrier. Rather, sit comfortably with your arms in your lap and your legs straight down or tucked under the chair a bit. Don't look away, look bored, or look around the room when someone is talking. Lean forward just a bit and make eye contact. Focus on the face of the speaker. Nod or smile in understanding.

In addition to body movement, pay attention to voice quality. Voice level, pitch, and fluency of speech communicate subtle messages. Listen to the voice quality of the person sharing to gain deeper insights into his feelings. And listen to your own voice quality and that of other members in the group as you respond. Voice level can show embarrassment, fear, uncertainty, or pride. Pitch may signal emotions, such as anger or frustration. Stuttering or hesitation gives clues to nervousness, embarrassment, anxiety, or lack of self-confidence. Listen to the voice level for the real meaning behind the words being spoken and behind the responses of group members.

And finally, take note of the environment. As the leader you'll have some influence on creating an environment conducive to sharing. Remember the important concept of "comfort zone." Different cultures have different comfort zones. In many cultures, such as Latin America, Indonesia, and India, it's customary for people to stand or sit very close together while talking. Not to do so is considered

See "Considerations on Meeting Space" in Chapter 5 for more on this topic.

disrespectful or rude. In the American culture, the comfort zone is about three feet, especially when standing. If people stand closer than that, we begin to squirm and back off. A sensitive leader will try to create an environment that respects the comfort zone of the members.

Setting the tone—respect. Respectful interactions communicate belief in the speaker. They affirm that the person speaking is trustworthy and can be responsible for his own life. Here are several indicators of respect:

A respectful listener will initially suspend all conclusions about the speaker. This means we set aside judgmental attitudes and stereotypes and that we don't label people. It also means that we don't impose our own feelings, beliefs, or values onto the speaker.

A respectful listener will take everything disclosed seriously. We need to avoid put-downs, even if we're only joking. We don't challenge the accuracy of the speaker's perceptions, nor do we attack.

A respectful listener will treat the speaker as an equal, regardless of how he perceives that person's worth to society or the group. We need to remember that God created each of us in His image. Therefore we must respect that image in each.

A respectful listener doesn't offer quick insights or answers to the speaker's concerns, but allows him to gain that insight himself. When we offer a quick fix, we communicate that we don't believe the person is smart enough to solve his or her own problems. Think how you feel when you've labored over an issue for a week, then someone hearing it for the first time tosses you a band-aid solution without even hearing the whole story.

A respectful listener shows genuine interest in the speaker and his concerns. This will usually grow as the group jells, but you need to model it.

A respectful listener stays on the topic the speaker initiates. Have you ever started voicing a concern, only to have the listener say, "Oh, I had an experience just like that! When I was working in Cleveland . . ."?

Suddenly the emphasis is off you and onto the other person. You feel cheated. Don't allow this to happen in your groups.

A respectful listener avoids being a rescuer. Our goal is to enable people to take the needed action on their own, with God's help. It is not to rescue them from all evil. Don't allow problem-solving to take the place of listening and praying in your group.

A respectful listener honors the speaker's ownership of the problem. The standard of ownership means that whatever a person discloses in the group belongs to him. No one else may discuss it outside of the group setting without the express permission of the sharer. Ownership also means that the sharer is the one who should initiate discussion about the issue outside of the group. Don't make the mistake—or allow others to make the mistake—of asking, "How's your love life?" or some equally embarrassing question at the Sunday-morning fellowship hour.

Some experts on group dynamics also maintain that the owner of the problem or issue is the only one who can initiate discussion of it in the group setting or privately. I disagree with this. There are many reasons why people hesitate to bring up a previously discussed problem. If we've agreed to be honest and accountable, we need to feel free to lovingly probe a tender area. We need to let our fellow members know that we care and are still available to help them.

A respectful listener maintains confidentiality. Since what is disclosed belongs to the discloser, that also means no one has permission to discuss the issue with anyone else, even another member of the group, without the express permission of the sharer. No one wants to feel that he is being talked about. No one wants to be the object of secret conclaves. And no one wants his innermost struggles shared with others, even as a prayer request.

Whatever you do, stress confidentiality in your groups. You won't have honesty and transparency without an ironclad guarantee that what is said within the group stays within the group.

"We are agents of Christ's authority, love, and grace—we *are* the Body of Christ. As His agents on Earth, we are called to show others the complete acceptance, love, and respect for sinners that Jesus showed to those around Him. Included in this respect and care is confidentiality. I cannot imagine Jesus telling others some juicy morsel of sin, even in the cause of 'prayer for the poor soul.'" —Gary Sweeten, *Breaking Free From the Past*

See "The Person Who Gossips" in Chapter 7 for more on this topic.

The flip side of confidentiality is trust. Group members must trust one another enough to be open and honest with one another. Stressing confidentiality is important, but you may need to go even further. Nick, a lay leader in his church, reports there are men he's worked with on various boards and committees with whom he refuses to be open and honest because he's been burned more than once by them. If Nick should end up in a group with one or more of these men, no amount of discussion about confidentiality will convince him that his deepest needs are safe in this group.

As the leader you need to pray for discernment and do your best to assess the trust level within the group. Probably the only solution is for the guilty party to confess his past failures, ask Nick's forgiveness, and promise confidentiality from this point forward.

Account-ability

✳

"So then, each of us will give an account of himself to God" (Romans 14:12)

It would be hard to say which of the seven key elements of a small group Bible study is the most important, but accountability has to rank pretty high. Often this one element makes the difference between a group in which people grow to maturity and one in which they don't.

Accountability is simply helping each person do what he or she has agreed to do to reach spiritual maturity. It's helping people become responsible for changing specific behaviors. And it grows out of transparency. Does it sound easy? If you think so you probably haven't been in a group with real accountability.

Accountability is costly—very costly. And it's scary. And difficult. And risky. Why? After all, don't people join groups to grow?

Some do; some don't. Some aren't sure. Many want to grow but aren't willing to pay the price. And even if they are sure, want to, and are willing to pay the price, growth is often difficult. If they could have grown in this area by themselves, they probably would have. If they've failed in the past, they may already be re-signed to failure in the future. Either way, your job is cut out for you.

Sometimes accountability will be natural because of the group's purpose or mission. For example, a group drawn together to conquer overeating may have as common goals to gain self-discipline over food, to develop new eating habits, and to lose a specific amount of weight. Within those broad goals each member may set personal specific goals. Sharon may decide to limit consumption of chocolate and to lose two pounds per week, while Valerie will stop snacking and lose three pounds per week.

In many groups, however, there is no common goal. Then each person must set one or more goals for himself, and each member of the group must find ways of helping the others meet their goals. The key to accountability is that the group member agrees to the goal and that the rest of the group agrees to monitor, encourage, assist, and if necessary, confront or rebuke to help him achieve success. Accountability is pro-viding the means to help you do what you say you'll do and to support you when you've failed. However, it doesn't allow members to continue making excuses or to say one thing and do another.

That's why it's costly. Even though everyone in the group affirms their commitment to accountability, when they are actually held accountable, they may respond with anger, denial, excuses, manipulation, or retribution.

Accountability answers the question, "How much do you really love the members of your group?" Ac-countability requires love, and love involves risk. You're risking your popularity as leader to insist on accountability. But it's worth it.

Accountability is like parental discipline. Kids complain about it, but when it's done properly and lovingly, they crave it because it shows that someone cares. And in today's society we all need someone to care for us. We need to know that our growth, our maturing process, is important to someone else.

The Sunday morning ministry of our singles group in San Francisco used a format where the people at each table of eight would discuss questions following the speaker's talk. In my early days as a discussion leader, my partner was a psychologist. As we studied together each week we'd decide on the action the passage called for. While some leaders simply discussed the theological implications of the lesson, we tended to bore in and encourage people to apply it.

No one at our table got away with flip answers or heady theology. We wanted application and accountability, even though we weren't a small group and had no guarantee of having the same people next week. The thing that amazed me was that our table always filled quickly, often with the same people. These were serious people who liked being held accountable as we followed up each week. They wanted to grow and recognized our table as one place that would contribute to that growth.

Some authorities on group dynamics use the term "confrontation" rather than "accountability." It's true that real accountability often requires a positive form of confrontation. Used this way, confrontation is "pointing out discrepancies in another person's walk or talk."*

*This definition of confrontation is from *Apples of Gold II: Speaking the Truth in Love,* by Gary Sweeten. Copyright © 1987 by Christian Information Committee, Cincinnati, OH

So if I say my goal is to lose two pounds per week, but I continue to snack on chocolate and potato chips every day, the people in my group should point out that discrepancy. This can be done lovingly but firmly. I need to account for my behavior. I need to explain the discrepancy. I either must change my goal or change my eating habits.

Many of us automatically shy away from confrontation. It scares us. It makes us uncomfortable. We're reluctant to risk our popularity. So we think about the discrepancy in another's behavior but never risk confronting. Such avoidance doesn't contribute to growth. Nor does it affirm the other person.

British psychiatrist Dr. Frank Lake noted that the amount of care and confrontation a person receives is equal to the growth and tribulation he or she will experience. In other words, growth is expensive. It's difficult. Its price is tribulation.

Dr. Lake points out that when people are not receiving good care and good confrontation, the small amounts of growth and tribulation that may result are not seen as gifts of God, but as burdens to be borne. He contends that the loving community of faith will provide a formula for growth: "maximum care + maximum confrontation = maximum growth + maximum tribulation." But Dr. Lake also points out that the "maximum tribulation" will be borne with a "minimum of murmuring" because the person knows he is loved and supported. However, if either side of the equation is missing (that is, either care or confrontation), then growth will be stifled.

If you fail to confront (or hold accountable) a group member about the discrepancies in his walk or talk, you may think you're avoiding immediate tribulation. You aren't risking yourself and maybe he'll figure it out on his own. But your failure to confront will lead to long-term pain and a lack of growth in the group member as well as guilt on your part for not doing what you knew was needed.

Setting the Pace

As with the other topics we've discussed, you as the leader will set the pace. If you ask the other members to hold you accountable to a specific goal each week, then faithfully report on your progress and gracefully accept accountability from them, you'll model the behavior you want the group as a whole to practice.

Just as Jesus modeled so much of the behavior He wanted from His disciples, you the leader must model accountability. Most groups will seek only the level of accountability the leader does. Once again, you must be vulnerable. You may even need to teach your group how to hold you accountable.

Another way you model for your group is how you hold the other members accountable. If you chasten or embarrass them expect them to do the same to one

"Agape love demands that we confront for the health and growth of the person confronted rather than satisfy our own needs for power, control, or even to show off our helping skills. Prior to using confrontation, ask yourself these key questions: Is this statement likely to help the person grow? Is this confrontation for them or for me? Are they ready to hear what I am about to say?" —Gary Sweeten, *Apples of Gold II*

another. If you lovingly point out the discrepancy between their words (their goals) and their actions (their actual behavior), they'll learn from you. If you leave each week with a mere, "I'll pray for you," that's what they'll do. If you ask, "How can I help you achieve this goal this week?" they'll learn from you.

The Bottom Line

Tough Love, a secular group that helps parents deal with out-of-control teens, has one of the better approaches to accountability that I've seen. The group is composed of parents trying to regain control over their teens or to regain normalcy in their homes in spite of teen rebellion. This is a group where everyone is dealing with the same general issue—teen rebellion—but very different individual issues. One may have a runaway child. Another has a drug abuser, while yet another has a son who is always in trouble with the law.

As parents begin to deal with their individual issues, they set a goal for handling their specific problem. The goal may be long-term or short-term, but it's one the parent feels will help his or her family cope with the situation.

Near the end of each meeting, the parents write down their "bottom line" on a paper supplied specifically for this purpose. The bottom line is one specific action the parent will take this week that will help them move toward the goal. The bottom line must be specific, measurable, and within the parent's ability to do without the cooperation of anyone else. Often it's one small step in the right direction. They don't try to tackle the whole problem in one week.

As each parent shares his bottom line with the group, another parent takes his name tag. In taking the name tag, the partner is committing to follow up, to hold the parent accountable for achieving the bottom line. The two determine how the partner can support the other, usually with a phone call to make sure the parent has taken the required action.

Note the elements your small group Bible study can

emulate. First, *the bottom line is one specific, measurable, and attainable action.* It's not some heavenly drivel like, "Spend more time with God." By the way it's worded you know for sure if you did it or didn't do it. Your bottom line might be to "Get up at 6:30 a.m. twice this week and spend 15 minutes reading my Bible and 15 minutes in prayer." That's specific. You know exactly what you've agreed to do. It's measurable. Either you do it or you don't. And it's attainable. It's not dependent on anyone else's cooperation. It's within your ability to accomplish without the help of anyone other than God. (That way, you can't blame anyone else if you fail.)

Second, *with the bottom line system someone else —a specific someone else—agrees to support you in your efforts.* What two days will you choose? Do you need a reminder Monday evening? Although that puts a bit of responsibility on the partner, the primary responsibility is still yours. But you know that someone else cares. A specific someone else is praying for you this week. Consider adapting the bottom line approach in your group.

> "Writing goals down tends to make them more concrete and specific and helps you probe below the surface of the same old clichés you've been telling yourself for years."
> —Alan Lakein, *How to Get Control of Your Time and Your Life*

Prayer
✳

> "Pray continually" (1 Thessalonians 5:17)

Bible studies are wonderful. Honestly sharing your deepest needs with others is both cathartic and useful. But if we expect to see real changes, real growth, real *teleios* in the members of our group, we need to pray!

We've already discussed the leader's responsibility to pray for the members of the group. But it's also important for the members of the group to pray for one another, both in the group meeting and during the week. Sometimes this comes naturally. Sometimes it's very difficult. But it's essential.

I find that the most difficult thing I must do as a leader is save time during each session to pray. And I must confess that I don't always succeed. It's so easy to get carried away discussing a great Bible study or allowing everyone to share their needs. More often than I want to admit, we finish sharing prayer needs just when it's time to leave. The best I can do is to encourage the members to pray for one another during the week. That's not an acceptable way to lead a group!

Be sure to see "The Person Who Won't Pray Aloud" in Chapter 7 for help in dealing with members who won't pray aloud.

The second most difficult thing for me to do as a leader is pray for my group members during the week. I've noticed that this is also a serious problem among most group members. I'm always amazed at how few people remember the prayer requests from week to week—which is my indicator of who's been praying and who hasn't. It's clear that the Enemy will do whatever is necessary to keep us from praying. So we must be sure our groups are praying.

Making Time for Prayer

You'd think it would be harder to make time for prayer in the early stages of the group when people are getting acquainted and need to give more background to their requests. But over the years I've found just the opposite. When a group begins, people are tentative. They share a little bit, see how it's accepted, then share a bit more the next week. It takes time for people to open up.

But the better the group members know one another the longer it takes to share. As people trust one another they disclose more parts of their lives. And as others pray for a specific need, they crave more information so they can pray even more effectively. As they begin to care about the person, they want to know how this issue is affecting other parts of his or her life. They're interested in the details. So it's easy to go from conveying a need in a few sentences to becoming a storyteller.

The difficulty is that the depth is good. We want people to feel free to share their lives, in detail if needed. We want members to care about the concerns of others. We want to be open, honest, transparent, vulnerable, and all the other great descriptives of good group life.

But if your group meets once a week for two hours and tries to incorporate all seven elements of a good small group Bible study, it's tough not to run out of time. And the part that usually gets short-changed is the group prayer time.

Let's look at some specific ways to cope with the time crunch.

Ask for wisdom. Let's not forget that our God is a problem-solving God. We're told in James 1:5, "If any of you lacks wisdom, he should ask God, who gives generously to all without finding fault, and it will be given to him." When you're stumped about how to save more time for prayer, ask God for wisdom and insight. He'll show you creative ways to accomplish your goal. After all, no one has more interest in having your group pray than He does!

Ask for help. I always admit to my group when I'm having trouble saving time for prayer. Of course they know it's a problem. We haven't had time to pray for three weeks—or is it four? But simply speaking the need helps make everyone aware of how they're contributing to the problem—or to the solution.

You need to be careful in doing this because it can have the effect of stifling disclosure. You don't want that! But I've found that I can open our time together by saying, "I'm concerned that we haven't had time for prayer in the past few weeks. Let's make an effort to get through the study and the sharing in time to allow at least ten minutes for prayer today." Then they're more careful in editing their comments to the essentials, and we do, in fact, have time to pray—that week, anyway.

Keep prayer requests immediate. One of my ground rules is that we limit prayer requests to the needs of the group members and members of their immediate families. I'm pretty strict about this policy.

During the first meeting we talk about sharing

> "The self-sufficient do not pray, the self-satisfied will not pray, the self-righteous cannot pray. No man is greater than his prayer life."
> —Leonard Ravenhill

needs and prayer support with one another. I'll say, "I know that from time to time, you'll want to pray for your great-aunt Martha in Cleveland. We want to pray with you for her needs because we care about you. But since we're limited in our time, please talk to one or more of us separately, outside of the regular group time, and we'll be glad to pray with you. Let's save our time in the group for personal needs, or the needs of people in your immediate household. That way everyone will have a chance to share and to have those needs prayed for by the others."

I've found that most people are pretty good about honoring that request. If it appears that, over time, several have forgotten, I'll mention it again during the administrative time in the group or speak privately to the chronic abuser. But I'll try not to embarrass someone by cutting them off as they're sharing a non-immediate request.

Keep prayer requests pertinent. Sometimes it's appropriate to limit prayer requests even more. If your group has a specific mission— dealing with substance abuse for example—you may want to limit disclosure and prayer to issues related to that mission.

The study itself may define the limits. When our women's group studied Joshua, we discussed his battles and the giants he conquered. We limited prayer requests to the "giants" each of us had identified in our own lives.

Again, you can handle prayer for additional needs before or after the meeting, at another time, or on the telephone. Here is where prayer partners are useful. If you limit what members can pray for in the group, assign prayer partners so each member has at least one person he or she can share needs with more extensively. That will also assure them that someone is praying for them daily.

You have one minute. One technique that's unpopular but effective is to announce at the beginning of the sharing time, "You each have one minute to bring

> "To pray together, in whatever tongue or ritual, is the most tender brotherhood of hope and sympathy that man can contract in this life." — Madame Anne Germaine de Staël, *Corinne*

us up to date or make a new prayer request. If we need more detail, you can add it during the prayer time."

Use this technique only when the group is cohesive, when members are already caring for one another outside of your weekly meeting, and when you know one another pretty well.

The advantage of this approach is that it makes people carefully edit their disclosure to the most pertinent points. The disadvantage is that it may limit someone who really needs to talk that day. But because the group is already caring for one another, it's pretty easy to spot such a need and agree to break the rules.

This approach also frees people from the need to talk if there's nothing new happening. I've heard people say, "No change from last week. Keep praying for my daughter. I'll give my minute to Linda so we can get more details on her need."

You won't want to use this technique often, but it is effective when you need a drastic change.

Share during prayer time. Sometimes our groups get into a rut where we disclose every detail of the need. Then we turn around and pray it all back to God, as if He hadn't been listening. While I personally prefer to pray for someone else in a group, sometimes we can share and pray at the same time by praying for our own need.

If time is short I'll ask the group to pray their own needs to God and add that we'll eavesdrop to get caught up. Their individual prayers bring us up to date and avoid the next problem.

> "He answered their prayers, because they trusted in him" (1 Chronicles 5:20).

Nix problem solving. One of the greatest tendencies of Christian groups is to turn the disclosure time into a counseling session. That's one reason we often don't have time to pray. We're too busy trying to solve the problem ourselves. I'm convinced that this is truly the work of the Enemy. Anything to keep us from praying!

I like to state the "no problem solving" guideline at the first meeting. Then, as soon as someone begins to offer advice, I remind them that we need to pray about the problem, not solve it.

This is important for a couple of reasons. First, when we problem solve, we're replacing God's perfect wisdom with our imperfect wisdom. It's a shortcut that results in the idolatry of humanism as we, in effect, make ourselves "like God."

See "Setting the tone—respect" in this chapter for more thoughts on respectful responses.

Second, when we try to give a quick answer (even if we're sure we know it), we're not showing respect for the other person. We need to let people know that we have faith in them to come to good solutions on their own, with the wisdom that only God can give. It's important for the leader to stop problem solving as soon as it begins and to maintain diligent watch over this barrier.

This prohibition would not apply to a need that can easily be resolved within the group. For example, John asks prayer for a car to commute to work because his won't run another mile. Henry just happens to have a spare car. Of course, he can offer it to John immediately, although they should work out the details after the group rather than taking group time to decide when and where John can get the car and how to handle insurance.

What we want to avoid is problem solving where Ted asks if John has called the church and Mark asks how far he needs to commute. Then Rod asks if John has tried getting his car fixed and Tim suggests his mechanic. These may be appropriate questions or comments, but they can be dealt with after the meeting.

Devote an entire meeting to sharing and praying. If yours is an ongoing group, it's wise to take a break from the study occasionally and devote an entire meeting to sharing and praying. During this meeting you can extend the worship period, give detailed attention to each person's sharing, and still have time for significant prayer—if you're careful.

Of course you'll still be tempted to let a particularly needy person go on and on. Or to let everyone go on and on. Or to problem solve. Or to do anything but pray. Don't give in to that temptation. Make it your goal to assure that the prayer time during this special meeting is the focal point.

Pray first. You may feel a little awkward, but one way to solve the "no time to pray" problem is simply to pray first. Again, you'll need to set some limits or you'll spend the entire meeting sharing and praying. But if you combine this with one or more of the other ideas in this section, you'll find that you not only have time for everything, but also that your prayer time is refreshed and renewed.

Pray in twos or threes. Sometimes it's effective to break your small group into smaller groups of two or three. You can do this before sharing prayer needs or after. Have each small group pray for their own needs, then if there's time, for other significant needs within the group. You won't want to use this technique all the time, but it's especially useful if there are several major needs to pray about.

Keep a Prayer Diary

As group members share their needs, be sure to keep a prayer diary. Regardless of its form, a prayer diary should include the date of the original request, the person making the request, the request itself, and the date answered.

As Ronald Klug affirms, "This is not a way of keeping score on God; it is a method of strengthening one's faith."* It's exciting to look back periodically and see just how many prayers God has answered. Sometimes we lose sight of His faithfulness as we continue adding to the list of needs.

There are at least two forms of prayer diaries that work well. The most common one is a chronological diary for the entire group. Many people actually use a ledger pad, but any notebook will do. You start the diary on the first day the group meets and add each request as it's spoken. So all the requests for one day

*Ronald Klug, *How to Keep a Spiritual Journal,* copyright © 1982, Thomas Nelson Publishers.

are together, identified by the person making the request. The next week, list new needs under that date. As people share praises and answers to their prayers, you note the date and cross it off.

I've recently started using another form of prayer diary that I like even better than the chronological one. It's a small three-ring binder, about five inches by three inches, with loose-leaf memo sheets. I use a separate page for each person in the group, as well as for anyone or anything else that I pray for regularly. It's helpful to use a tabbed divider for your group so you can turn to the right section quickly. As each person shares, you turn to his or her page in the book and add the date and the new prayer requests. When a prayer is answered, I note it with the date.

This diary has the advantage of keeping all of one person's needs together so I can really dig in and pray diligently. It also keeps each person's information together, so it's easy to see the history at a glance. And I often have less writing to do, since the details from previous weeks are easy to find. Also, I find that I pray for my group members more often using this system. Since it fits into my purse (or into a man's suit pocket), I carry it with me most of the time. Then I can use spare moments of driving or waiting to pray for my group.

I like to use a multi-colored pen on my prayer diary, so I can write the date answered in red. If someone in the group is feeling discouraged, it's particularly effective to hold up a page full of red marks!

"We should have a definite list of those for whom we intercede. It is better to pray daily for a few than only infrequently for many. It is God himself who gives us those for whom we are to intercede. A special part of his universe he entrusts to our care, and for that part we are to pray." — Charles F. Whitson, *Instructions in the Life of Prayer*

CHAPTER 4

Learning by the Book

WE'VE DISCUSSED THE importance of using the Bible as our source document. We agreed that a small group Bible study should definitely study the Bible. But does that mean you must use only the Bible? Must you write the study guide or teach the group from your own personal study? Of course not. If we meant that we'd immediately disqualify most readers of this book —and most of the Bible study leaders in the country. Few people have the time, the interest, the skills, or the gifts to develop excellent study guides for use in a small group Bible study.

So what do you do? You look at the published study guides that are available and evaluate them. Because you know the general needs of your group— or potential group—you'll automatically eliminate many

"All Scripture is God-breathed and is useful for teaching, rebuking, correcting, and training in righteousness" (2 Timothy 3:16)

of the available guides. They'll be too deep or too basic. They'll be aimed at the wrong sex, age, or life needs. They'll take too much or too little time. The elimination is easy. But how do you select from those remaining?

Is It Biblically Sound?

✲

The information in this section is from *Toward an Exegetical Theology* by Walter Kaiser (Baker Book House) and *Keys to Understanding and Teaching Your Bible* by Thomas E. Fountain (Thomas Nelson Publishers).

Even more important than finding a study that is right for your group is finding a study guide that is hermeneutically correct. (One friend said, "Herman who?")

Hermeneutics is the science and methodology of Scripture interpretation. Simply stated, hermeneutics uses good inductive Bible study techniques.

Inductive Bible study is a reasoning process that proceeds from basic facts to conclusions. It's a process that's consistent with the way people normally solve problems and study new ideas. The alternative is deductive reasoning, which is the logic of proof. Deductive reasoning begins with a hypothesis that the student wants to prove.

So in inductive Bible study, you begin with the various facts and use them to draw a conclusion. In deductive study, you begin with a conclusion and then look for facts that will support that argument. While the deductive approach is useful, especially for systematic theology, the inductive approach is a better and safer one for those of us who aren't Bible scholars.

One of the more common hermeneutical approaches to inductive Bible study is the "grammatico-historical method" that originated during the reformation years, but was described and named by Karl A. G. Keil in 1788. Experts still consider this approach as the foundation of biblical interpretation today. This method aims to determine the sense of a passage through 1) the laws of grammar, and 2) the facts of history.

Understand the Grammar

The grammatico-historical technique looks first at the grammar of the text. It assumes that, since the Bible is written communication, we must therefore seek to understand the simple, direct, plain, ordinary, and literal sense of the words, phrases, clauses, and sentences. But it also recognizes that the biblical languages have several distinctions from English.

- For example, the Bible is ancient. The oldest books of the Old Testament were written at least 3600 years ago. The New Testament is almost 2000 years old.
- Contemporary America is separated from the part of the world where the biblical events took place by thousands of miles, by cultures, and by a mindset distinctly different from ours.
- Two of the three languages in which the Bible was written are dead languages. Furthermore, neither Hebrew, Aramaic, nor Greek are part of the Germanic family of languages to which English belongs. Thus they have only the most remote connections with English.
- Many of the words and phrases in these languages were more specific than our English words. In addition, they were often more picturesque than English, carrying a depth of meaning that we can only appreciate by doing a word study in the original language.

However, even acknowledging these distinctives, this approach assumes that anyone can understand the message of the Bible.

> "The Bible was never intended to be a book for scholars and specialists only. From the very beginning it was intended to be everybody's book, and that is what it continues to be."
> —F. F. Bruce

Understand the History

The second part of the grammatico-historical approach is an understanding of history. This includes a careful consideration of the time and circumstances in which the author wrote, and the specific meaning that author's words require when examining the historical context and background.

"The Bible is a harp with a thousand strings. Play on one to the exclusion of its relationship to the others, and you will develop discord. Play on all of them, keeping them in their places in the divine scale, and you will hear heavenly music all the time."
—William P. White

The historical approach suggests the importance of two elements of study. First, it's essential to analyze and understand the author's intent or purpose for writing the book. Intimately linked to this is the original reader's or recipient's need, which is clarified by understanding the historical context. Sometimes the intent is stated, as in John 20:31. In other books you must dig it out by careful study.

Next, it's essential to analyze the passage in the context of the rest of the book, all of Scripture, and the canon of theology generally accepted by the Christian church. This is an essential but often overlooked element of most study guides. If the author has taken verses out of context to prove a point you can be sure that the study guide is suspect.

This is not to say that an author can't use a verse from one book to interpret or give weight to another passage. In fact, if it's used in the right context, it should be cited. But be sure to read the surrounding verses to determine that the context allows for the interpretation the study guide author is giving.

Let's Get Practical

∗

Walter C. Kaiser, Jr., vice president of education at Trinity Evangelical Divinity School, affirms the grammatico-historical approach. But he says that it fails to go far enough. It doesn't map the route, he claims, between determining the authentic meaning of a passage and delivering that meaning to modern men and women who want it translated into some kind of significance in their lives.

This results, he says, in dry, technically correct sermons or studies that have no meaning to the audience. To solve this problem, he has coined the "syntactical-theological method." The syntax includes all the elements of the grammatico-historical method, as described above. The theological study moves from the sterile recitation of a technically proper analysis to a doctrinally and theologically correct, but also meaningful, message for the student.

This concept is essential for any leader searching for a good study guide. In addition to assuring that it's doctrinally and theologically correct, be sure that it's meaningful!

When I'm looking for a Bible study guide, I want one that is not only technically correct, but one that also brings the text to life through practical examples and meaningful application. I want a guide that seeks to contribute to measurable spiritual growth as a primary aim.

Finally, I'd encourage any Bible study leader to read books on hermeneutics and theology from time to time. Yes, they are difficult for the novice to plow through. But they'll add much to your ability to be a good leader. Appendix A suggests several resources that are readable by non-theologians.

Give Me a Good Question!
✳

Questions form the skeleton of most Bible study guides. The best study guides boast a strong structural framework of good questions. But what makes a good question? One that fulfills several goals. Let's examine each of these.

A good question creates or maintains interest. It keeps the attention and interest of the reader. There needs to be enough variety in type and format so the study avoids taking on a sing-song feeling. A good question keeps the reader awake.

A good question moves the student to the next question. It goes someplace. It's not an end in itself. It's like an escalator; it moves the student from one level to the next. A good question keeps the reader asking for more.

A good question serves a useful purpose in the overall plan of the study. It contributes to the theme or purpose of the study. It moves the reader's attention

In this section we'll look at evaluating written questions that make up Bible study guides. In the next chapter we'll look at verbal questions and their role in guiding the discussion during the group meeting.

toward the logical conclusion. It isn't thrown in just because it's there. A good question keeps the reader on track.

A good question respects the reader's intelligence. It affirms that the student is an adult with an average level of intelligence. It avoids the obvious, such as, "What did Jesus say in verse 3?" A good question keeps the reader thinking.

A good question causes the student to seek or see a personal application. It leads the reader to an "Aha!" experience. It either points to or points out a way the reader can integrate this passage into his or her life. A good question keeps the reader applying the Word of Truth to real, common, everyday life.

Four Types of Questions

There are four general types of questions. Good Bible study guides use all four in each lesson. The best study guides maintain the students' interest by sprinkling the last three types throughout the study in a way that keeps the readers on their toes.

Let's look at these four types of questions and why they're important to excellence in your small group Bible study. If the study guide you choose doesn't include all these types of questions, you may need to supplement it. You can add the ones that are lacking and use them in your discussion group. Or you may want to save yourself the effort and be sure that the study guide you select includes the right mix of each.

Break the ice. The icebreaker is the first question or two in each chapter. It serves two purposes.

First, it focuses the student's thinking toward the topic and creates a need for the lesson in the mind of the reader. It draws the reader's attention away from the hundred other distractions he or she faces and to the topic at hand in a casual, non-threatening way. And it gives him or her a present-day, real-life reason to continue the study.

Second, it's useful to you as the leader, especially when your group is new. An icebreaker question helps draw your group's attention to the lesson. If the group is still a bit uncomfortable with one another, it gives you a non-threatening question to ask that has no right or wrong answer. It gets people used to hearing their own voices and the voices of others in this setting today.

Because of this, look for study guides with icebreakers that are related to the lesson, but that are not too personal or probing, especially early in the life of the group. Good icebreakers can be answered in a various ways, from flippantly to seriously. They allow a lot of room for personal interpretation. And the responses can give you as the leader a lot of insight into the hearts and minds of your group members.

After your group has jelled, you may decide to ignore the icebreaker during your discussion and jump right into the heart of the study. That's fine. The icebreaker already served its purpose when the members did their homework. However, even in a cohesive group, don't ignore the need to focus on the subject of the day. The NIV Serendipity Bible for Groups provides excellent icebreakers for every passage of the Bible (see Appendix A, "Resources for Leaders," for details).

Here's an example of an icebreaker: "How do you know when someone really loves you?" One person, rolling her eyes romantically, may say, "When he brings me flowers!" Another may smile and say, "When she scratches my back." Still another, a more serious member, may say, "Joe showed me his love when he gave up watching the game to install my new garbage disposal." And your super-spiritual member will go right to the theology and quote 1 John 4:10: "This is love: not that we loved God, but that he loved us and sent his Son as an atoning sacrifice for our sins." But regardless of the answer, the icebreaker has directed everyone's attention to love and specific ways to identify it.

> "There is only one meaning for every place in Scripture. Otherwise the meaning of Scripture would not only be unclear and uncertain, but there would be no meaning at all—for anything which does not mean one thing surely means nothing."
> —William Ames

What does it say? The observation question simply asks, "What does the text say?" It usually has a single right answer that is clear from the passage.

Observation questions are the stuff of which most Bible study guides are made. In fact, over 90 percent of the questions in many published studies are observation questions. They'll bore your group to mutiny unless they're carefully and cleverly written. Look for study guides that ask observation questions without always saying, "What does verse 14 say?" Ugh! Such questions insult the intelligence of your group.

"It is impossible to mentally or socially enslave a Bible-reading people."
—Horace Greeley

I had this experience in leading a women's Bible study one year. We had chosen a book from one of the nation's largest study guide publishers. Most of the questions were observation, with one application question at the end of the lesson. The author had not been creative in writing the questions and I was still enough of a novice that I simply asked the questions one after another. I knew the group was getting bored, but I wasn't sure why.

One day a member called and said, "Pat, I'm quitting the Bible study. I can't take that book one more week. It's so boring!"

"Paula," I said, after we had discussed it a bit more, "You're absolutely right. I knew there was a problem, but I couldn't identify it. Let me make you a deal. You stay in the group and continue doing your homework in the book, but when we get to the group, we won't discuss those questions. I'll write some questions that will help us understand the passage and really apply it to our lives. Would that make a difference?"

She agreed to give it a try. I had my work cut out for me. I wrote the new questions and presented them to the rest of the group the next week. All quickly agreed that they'd be a lot more motivated to come if we used these new questions. Soon several other small groups doing the same study began using the revised questions.

Now don't get me wrong. A study needs observation questions. They direct the student's attention to the Bible text and move the study in a definite direction. They clarify what the passage says and what it doesn't say. But like white bread, they get boring if that's all there is. So look for a study that uses observation questions sparingly (no more than one third of most lessons) and words them creatively.

Here's a well-written observation question: "Read Matthew 22:34-40, Deuteronomy 6:5, and Leviticus 19:18. Summarize the two greatest commandments." Note there is one right answer that is clear from the three texts. But it's vastly superior to, "What do Matthew 22:34-40, Deuteronomy 6:5, and Leviticus 19:18 say?" That's boring and insulting to the intelligence of the reader.

Here's another good observation question: "On the night before He was to suffer and die on the cross, Jesus explained and clarified the second of these commandments. Read John 13:34. How does this new commandment differ from the old commandment?" Again, this calls the reader to observe, then make a comparison between two knowns. There is a right answer. Readers are smart enough to find it. And this observation question leads naturally to the next kind of question.

"The first thing I've discovered . . . is don't ask a question with a right answer. The worst offender is one that can be answered with a simple yes or no." —Em Griffin, *Getting Together: A Guide for Good Groups*

What does it mean? The next type of question is the interpretation question, which asks, "What does the text mean?" Although each passage has only one meaning, that meaning is not necessarily obvious from the text. Interpretation questions may require some additional digging. This is where the grammatico-historical approach serves you. You may need to understand the passage within the context of the book or the whole of Scripture. You may need to do a word study on a specific Greek or Hebrew expression. You may need to use a Bible dictionary or other resource to understand the cultural setting. Or you may need to synthesize the answers from two or three preceding observation questions to draw the true meaning from the text.

Interpretation questions often ask "how?" "why?" or "what do you think?" Observation questions, by contrast, usually ask, "what?" or "when?" Interpretation questions add a bit of meat to that white bread. They should make up about one third of the study.

Here's an example of an interpretation question: "How does fulfilling this new commandment fulfill the first and greatest commandment?" Although the answer is pretty easy, it does take some understanding to bridge the gap between the two. And the text doesn't give the answer.

"With this new command, was Jesus raising or lowering the standard for believers? Explain." This is a "what do you think?" type of question. It stretches the reader by requiring an explanation.

Interpretation questions are the meat of a good Bible study. They draw you into the text in new, creative ways. They make you think. And they're the bridge between observation and application.

Who cares? The final type of question is the application question. This question asks, "Who cares?" or "What I must do about it?" The answer may be implied from the text, but it requires the student to get personal.

Application questions are, in my mind, the key to a good Bible study. Unfortunately, they're the weakest element of most studies. All too many Bible study guides spend 95 percent of their time on observation and interpretation, leaving only the last question or two for "Putting it to Work" or "Summing Up." It's been my experience that most discussion groups don't get to the last question, leaving the members with a boring, meaningless, academic study—just the type Walter Kaiser warned against. Such studies don't bear fruit; they don't result in changed lives.

I prefer to see application woven throughout the study. Look for studies that ask a couple of observation questions, a couple of interpretation questions, then a couple of penetrating application questions. In effect, such a study says, "Here's what the Bible says, this is what it means, and here is how I will apply that lesson to my life."

Don't be afraid of application questions that get personal. Many studies actually list such questions as personal and warn the leader not to ask them in the group setting. I believe this short-changes your group. People today are looking for meaning in life. Go ahead and ask the tough questions. Go ahead and probe a bit after your group has developed some trust. Go ahead and follow up on trite answers. Gently and lovingly prod your group members to growth-oriented application and accountability.

Here's an example of good application questions: "What are some practical ways you can show love to one another? Which of these are easy for you? Which involve sacrifices? What are some obstacles you find in loving others?" These questions are direct. They're personal. They ask for a commitment. They probe feelings, motivations, and obstacles. They're pretty tough to ignore. And they result in people looking deeply enough to allow the Holy Spirit to call them to repentance and change.

The reason I began writing Bible studies was to make them meaningful to people. The reason I continue is because I've seen the lives that have been changed when people get serious about applying the Word of God to the common, everyday parts of their lives. If the study guide you choose is short on application, you may as well stay home and watch TV.

Topical or Book Study?
✳

One question many leaders ask is whether they should do a topical study or a book (of the Bible) study. Both are valuable when done correctly. Both can contribute to spiritual growth if they focus on application.

The advantage of studying through a book of the Bible is that the study guide usually follows a good inductive approach and doesn't take verses or passages out of context. You gain an overall understanding of the needs of one particular group of people (the original audience) and how those needs were met by God as He used an inspired author. As you complete several such studies, your group members will gain a good facility with the Bible, or at least with the portions studied.

The disadvantage of most book studies is that they may or may not hit a "need nerve" with the members of your group. Because our society is so consumed with the "what's in it for me" attitude, some people will find a book study boring. They want to see how their study relates to their lives right now.

Therefore, the trend today is toward topical studies. Numbed by the popularity of the many self-help and topic-specific books on the market, many people seek a Bible study that will address a specific need in their lives with precise biblical helps. That's fine, as long as it doesn't violate the criteria for good inductive Bible study.

The major advantage of a topical study is that it scratches where people itch. It targets a specific need and gives answers from the whole counsel of God. And if done well it can give your group members a broader knowledge of Scripture in a shorter time than can single book studies.

The major weakness in many topical studies is that they use the deductive approach. I call this the "prooftext" approach. In this system, the author begins with a premise—that God wants every believer to pray, for example. Then the author sends you scampering all over Scripture looking up a dozen or more verses that relate to God's desire that we pray. You don't delve into any one passage, nor do you study the passages in context. You simply prove that the author's original hypothesis is true.

In such studies the responsibility falls on the leader to be sure that the author hasn't taken the passages out of context or given them a meaning that a deeper grammatical or historical analysis would invalidate. If you're not personally well-versed in Bible interpretation, a poorly researched study can take your lambs down a pretty thorny path of error.

A common complaint of many doing such a topical study is that by the time they've flipped to several verses in the Old and New Testaments, they've lost their train of thought. Many today are simply unable to take six to eight different but related ideas and draw a unified conclusion from them. Deductive topical studies will leave such persons dissatisfied and frustrated.

Furthermore, many such studies are 90 percent observation and 10 percent (or less) application. About all they do is test your skills at finding your way around the Bible. They don't help you develop an idea, nor do they give you a solid understanding of any passage.

> "Apply yourself to the whole text, and apply the whole text to yourself."
> —Johannes Albrecht Bengel

Not all topical studies have these weaknesses, so we don't want to cast them all in the same suspicious mold. Many topical studies focus on one major passage per lesson, although they may support that passage with other appropriately related texts. The authors are careful not to take proof-texts out of context, but rather, to delve deeply enough for the student to understand the connection. And while the author may have had an original hypothesis, he starts with the Word of God and allows it to point to the truth rather than making the Word prove his theory.

Regardless of whether you select a book or a topical study guide, and an inductive or deductive approach, be sure that the author supports the questions with evidence from other passages. This is a good way of assuring that the author isn't developing a whole new theology based on one passage.

So whether you choose to study a book of the Bible or a topic, consider these criteria carefully. A good study guide will make your life as a leader so much easier!

The Importance of a Leaders' Guide

✳

If you're a new leader you'll especially appreciate a good leaders' guide. Even if you're experienced it never hurts to know what the writer had in mind. And it's always fun to have a few extra tidbits to share with your group. That's why I like studies with a good leaders' guide.

Different publishers have different philosophies about leaders' guides. Some have none; some have a limited guide at the back of the book. Some have a separate book you can buy.

In the Bible study guides I've written I provide an extensive leaders' guide at the back of the book. This means you don't have to buy a separate leaders' guide, but you get as much information as if you had. It also means that diligent members of the group will have as much information as the leader and can therefore gain the maximum from each lesson, even if they have to miss a group meeting.

Although the author can't meet with each of you before your meetings, the leaders' guide will give you his or her insights. It can clear up potential questions, give you additional resources, and offer suggestions for guiding the discussion. Of course, if there's too much information you can always skip it. But it's there if you want to check your responses.

Regardless of whose study guides you use, you'll find that a good leaders' guide makes your life a whole lot easier.

Obtaining Copies of the Study Guide

*

It's important to plan your group far enough ahead to allow time to obtain copies of the study guide. The best place to look for study guides that meet your criteria is in your local Christian bookstore. Often, if you explain to the owners that you're starting a small group and are looking for just the right study guide, they'll allow you to take several on consignment. That will give you time to review them more thoroughly at home, then return those that don't meet your needs. It will also allow you to show them to others who may be part of the decision-making process.

It's a good idea to select your study guide at least a month before the group is to begin. This is particularly true if you'll need more copies than the bookstore typically stocks. You'll need some idea of how many copies you want the store to order. They'll appreciate it if you can give them an estimate so they can order the guides all at once rather than making a special order for each member who wanders in over the next month looking for the same book. In fact, many bookstore owners prefer to order a few too many copies. It's easier to return unsold copies than to make small special rush orders.

You can handle the study guides in one of two ways. After telling the owner how many you'll need, you can have each member go to the bookstore to buy his or her copy. Sometimes that's a hassle, especially if members of your group work during the day or if the bookstore is not conveniently located.

The other option is for you or someone in your group to buy all of them and resell them to each member. Sometimes the store will even put them on account so you don't have to come up with the cash in advance. This is particularly true if your church has an account at the store or if the owners get to know you.

Often, if you order several books they'll give you a discount, making the study guides even more affordable for each member. And many stores will allow you to return unused study guides within a reasonable time.

If you don't know how many will be in your group (a large Bible study, for example), order about 10 percent more books than you expect to need. Make sure you can return the unsold ones. Then calculate the cost, either retail or discounted, including applicable state and local taxes, and sell one to each member.

Another option is to order your study guides through one of the many discount mail order catalogs specializing in Christian books. Many offer a better selection than some of the smaller Christian bookstores and some offer excellent delivery times. You may have problems with trying to return unsold books, though.

The same is true for Christian publishers. You can order directly from them. However, this isn't as convenient and may not be as flexible for you. Some publishers require a minimum purchase and a financial statement for credit. So unless you have some extraordinary need that requires using one of these alternatives, you're better off sticking to your local Christian bookstore for your study guides.

CHAPTER 5

Before You Begin

SO FAR WE'VE talked about theory. Now let's switch gears and get very practical. Some of you are already leading groups and have come to this book looking for new ideas. Others have never led a group and by now are feeling a bit overwhelmed. Where do you begin?

Let's take the person who's never led a group. Perhaps you've noticed a need among some people in your church. Maybe the moms of preschoolers need a Bible study. Or perhaps it's the dads of teens. Possibly you and several friends want to deal with overeating or co-dependency from a biblical perspective. Or perhaps your minister asked you to start a small group Bible study for the college-age members of your church. Whatever the situation, you've now recognized a need. What next?

"Suppose one of you wants to build a tower. Will he not first sit down and estimate the cost to see if he has enough money to complete it?" (Luke 14:28).

It's Time to Pray

✳

"Unless the Lord builds the house, its builders labor in vain" (Psalm 127:1).

Whether leading a small group was your idea or someone else suggested it to you, your first step is to see what the Lord has to say. Is now the time for this group? Are there special circumstances you should consider? Are you the person to lead it?

When I'm about to make a decision like this I always seek the prayer support of several friends, especially if I have strong feelings one way or the other. Since God isn't in the habit of speaking audibly to me, I need the objectivity of someone who has less emotion invested in the decision. Together and separately we'll pray for wisdom and guidance.

No one can tell you how to pray or how long to wait for an answer. If you're ready to be a leader, you'll know that. But it's not a good idea to begin an endeavor like this without being sure that the Lord is walking before you.

The Ministry of the Co-leader

✳

"So for a whole year Barnabas and Saul met with the church and taught great numbers of people" (Acts 11:26).

Once you've clearly defined your group and made a commitment to lead it, the next question is, "Can I handle it alone?" If you have a choice, answer "No!"

A co-leader can either serve as an assistant to you or as one who almost equally shares the load. How you decide this will depend on your own skills, interests, and available time. The key is to be sure that you've communicated clearly and that both of you agree on what each will do.

I'm a firm believer in co-leaders or assistant leaders, for several reasons. A co-leader can provide you with a perspective that alone you'll probably miss. Leading a group can take a lot of attention to stay on track. A co-leader can pick up on needs through comments or body language that may fly right by you.

A co-leader is essential if you have a mixed group; if the leader is a man, the co-leader should be a woman, and if the leader is a woman, the co-leader should be a man. I'll go into the reasons for that later.

A co-leader can monitor your timing, signaling you when it's time to cut off the study and move on to prayer requests and prayer. Sometimes when I'm in the midst of a good study I forget all about the time. I need a good co-leader to wave her arms at me and insist that we simply must stop.

A co-leader can fill in the awkward gaps or re-phrase a question when necessary. This is especially important early in the life of a group when people may still be reluctant to answer. The co-leader can also help you set the pace for openness and vulnerability.

A co-leader can relieve you of much of the respon-sibility for follow-up and other personal contact with members of the group. Note that I said much, not all. You'll still need to make some phone calls and stay in touch. But your co-leader can take the bulk of that responsibility.

Your co-leader can take over if you're sick, out of town, or can't attend for any other reason. Your group will flounder much less if they know that someone is still in charge when you aren't there.

Perhaps most important, this year's co-leader is next year's leader. I'm a firm believer in always hav-ing leaders "in training." Wouldn't your life be calmer now if you had been able to co-lead for a year before taking on your own group? Co-leading is where many people gain the confidence to become leaders. Reread Acts 11:26. Note who the leader was and who the assistant was. You know how that changed over time.

Don't be threatened by an excellent co-leader. Be grateful. Share as much of the leadership as possible with that person. Encourage him or her to branch out and lead a new group next year. The church never has enough people who are willing to be leaders. There will never be more leaders than there are Bible studies to go around, so you need not fear for your position. Simply divide and multiply!

What to Look for in a Co-leader

Who would be a good co-leader? Begin by looking at the list of leadership qualifications in Chapter 2. Your co-leader should have most, if not all, of those qualities. However, they may be dormant or under-developed. Your mission, should you decide to accept it, is to identify potential—and then to help that potential develop into leadership.

Next you'll want to try to select someone you feel has gifts, talents, or strengths that complement yours. For example, I hate making phone calls, so I like to choose a friendly co-leader who likes and has time for personal follow-up.

Be aware, however, that since your co-leader is your counterpart, he may not be your best friend. In fact, you may find yourself frustrated at times with the very assets you selected the person for. It's a lot like marriage. Those aspects of your partner that best counterbalance your weaknesses may be the very ones that drive you crazy!

If your group will include only men or only women, your choice is obvious. If, however, you've decided on a mixed group, I strongly recommend that you choose a co-leader of the opposite sex. This may be your wife (or husband), or it may be someone else.

Our singles group had a male leader and a female co-leader for each discussion table and for most mixed groups. It worked well because the co-leader, usually female, was often more intuitive and could pick up on subtle needs or body language that raced right past many of the men. The co-leader was also freer to focus on a need that the leader was missing by simply saying, "Wait a minute. I think Ruth is trying to make a different point." Or, "Tom, how do you feel about what Jill said?" Discussions became much more meaningful with a perceptive co-leader.

I've been part of geographically situated Bible study groups that include both couples and singles from that area. Each group had a leader and a co-leader—both men. I was often frustrated to see what was to most of the women very clear nonverbal communication—or

> "Light is the task where many share in the toil."
> —Homer

> "It is when we work with others as teams, when each one is contributing his own distinctive gifts, service, and effort that the function of the body, and the purpose of the gifts is accomplished."
> —Lawrence Richards and Gib Martin, *A Theology of Personal Ministry*

Who Does What?

Leader	Co-leader
• Prepares for and leads discussion	• Prepares for and helps lead discussion. Leads in the absence of the leader or as agreed upon with the leader.
• Asks most of the questions in the discussion. Sets the primary direction or goal of the discussion.	• Rephrases or clarifies questions as needed. Asks follow-up questions to pursue a point or meet a special need.
• Paces discussion, disclosure, and prayer to allow adequate time for each.	• Monitors time and warns leader if any portion is exceeding the allowed time.
• Keeps discussion on track.	• Helps keep discussion on track by rephrasing or by pointing out a digression.
• Follows up on some members each week, particularly those who are struggling.	• Follows up on all absentees each week, as well as members known to be struggling or in need.
• May assume responsibility for socials or fellowship.	• May assume responsibility for socials or fellowship.
• Prays regularly for each person in the group.	• Prays regularly for each person in the group.

even verbal communication—flying right by both male leaders. These groups could have been much more effective by tapping into the God-given strengths of both sexes.

> "God has so ordered that men, being in need of each other, should learn to love each other, and bear each other's burdens."
> —Sala

Roles and Responsibilities

If you have a co-leader you need to be clear on the division of labor. Otherwise you may run into conflict. Generally I divide the roles and responsibilities of the leader and co-leader as shown on the previous page.

Note that this is only one of many possible models. Again, whatever works for both you and your co-leader will be fine. The key is to be sure that you both understand and agree on the division of labor and responsibility.

What About Rotating Leadership?

✳

Some Bible studies are organized with rotating leadership. Using this plan a different person leads each lesson, set of lessons, unit, or time period. The rotation is usually agreed upon early in the life of the group.

This system often works very well. It gives more people the opportunity to lead a study and probably gives each person a greater respect for the effort a leader puts into preparation. Certainly it's more difficult to criticize a leader if you know you're up next!

If you decide on rotating leadership you may still want someone to take on overall leadership for the group and make sure that it's developing as the members had hoped. I've seen groups with rotating leadership flounder when no one had ultimate responsibility for the group. Often in this case, the person with the gift of leadership emerges as the informal leader, if not the designated leader. You definitely need good communication within the group so problems are identified and dealt with before they become major.

Once you've determined the type of group you want, considered the preliminary details, and invited your co-leader, it's time to find the rest of the group.

This may already be done for you if you're assuming an existing group, or it may take some initiative on your part. Either way the key is for you as the leader to be interested in and to show genuine concern for each person. Otherwise you'll appear only to care for them as members or potential members of your group.

Let's look at the different ways to invite people to join your small group Bible study and see which might work best for each type of group.

Make a personal invitation or phone call to each prospective member. This approach works best for a small group that will meet in a home and will be limited in both number and type of participants. We used this type of invitation for our "How to Be Happy Though Single" group because we wanted an equal number of men and women, and were looking for people who could make specific contributions or whom we felt had specific needs.

If this is your only approach, plan on calling at least twice as many people as you have space for. People are busy, and even those who want to join the group may not be able to come when you've scheduled it. You may also want to use this approach in addition to the other types of invitations we'll discuss.

Put a notice in your church bulletin or group newsletter. This approach is effective in gaining the attention of many members. It's effective for a larger study that is open to anyone meeting the criteria (women, men, moms, substance abusers). People can sign up as directed in the announcement. You can limit enrollment to the number of spaces available.

We used this method for our women's ministries Bible studies. We usually had three different large groups available, each meeting at a different time and

Recruiting Members for the Group

∗

"'Come, follow me,' Jesus said" (Matthew 4:19)

targeting a different group (moms at home, women working outside the home, and older women at home). Within the larger groups there were several small groups.

If you use this approach plan on running the notice for at least two weeks, preferably more. With illness and our busy lives, it's easy for people to miss an announcement given only once.

Make an announcement from the pulpit. This approach works well with the bulletin notice. It's especially useful if the larger study is available to everyone in the congregation, or at least to a large constituency.

Our church uses this approach, in addition to bulletin announcements and fliers, to promote the community groups. In fact, in addition to an announcement, the minister often interviews people who have been members of the groups and benefited from them, adding a little drama and a personal touch.

Distribute fliers. This approach is usually a supplement to all of the above, even the phone call. People like to have something tangible they can read, review, and consider. A flier allows you to provide all of the pertinent information in one easily readable format. You can even include a tear-off registration form at the bottom.

Before you print it, have several people read the flier to make sure that it's clear, readable, and free from errors; and that it communicates what you want it to. Add some art work. Use clip art if you aren't artistic, but make sure that it's quality. It may be the first impression your group makes on potential members.

Regardless of the approach or approaches you use, make sure to tell people everything they need to know. Make sure they're aware, for example, of what the study will entail. If possible, give the name of the study, the author, and why you selected it. What benefits can the member expect by joining this group? Also be clear about the homework requirements. Using the discussion approach, members must prepare their lessons in advance. How much time each week can they expect to spend on homework and how much in the group itself?

Tell people who will be in the group. You may or may not know each member yet, but at least indicate the targeted group. Will there be only male executives who work downtown—or is the group open to any man who's free for breakfast on Tuesday? Will it include only alcoholics or all substance abusers? What about their spouses? The targeted make-up of the group will help potential members make their decisions.

Make sure people know when and where the study will meet. This makes a big difference to busy Americans. Most will need to check their calendars to determine if they're free on Wednesday evening. And how far away is it? What will that mean in terms of transportation? Some people aren't willing to travel more than a few minutes. Others don't mind a longer commute, especially if the group will meet a significant felt need.

Tell prospective members how long the group will continue. They want to know what they're committing to. How many weeks will the group meet, and how long will each session last?

Are there attendance requirements? I hope by now you've realized how important attendance is. But what are you willing to live with? The answer to that question may depend on the type of group you're starting. And it may limit who can participate. If Jerry has a

Information Potential Members Need to Know

*

"Before you invite anyone to join your small group, make sure that you know and can communicate clearly what your group will do and what is being asked of participants. Common understanding develops when sufficient time is taken to think and talk through what this particular small group is all about so that everyone understands. Defining terms is very helpful. Time taken to work on the promises that the group members make is

time that allows the group organizers, and then the group itself, to focus on its reasons for meeting, and to become a more satisfying experience for all those involved."
—Roberta Hestenes, *Using the Bible in Groups*

vacation planned right in the middle of the study, is that OK? If a mom with three preschoolers can't commit to perfect attendance, can you live with that? You need to decide on your expectations before you invite people to join.

The more you communicate in the beginning—before people sign up—the fewer misunderstandings you'll have later. It's worth the time it takes!

As an alternative you may want to reserve some of these decisions for the group as a whole to make. That's fine for those decisions where you have some flexibility. It may work even better in some cases. But be prepared for some changes in the direction you had originally planned. Plan your schedule so you can spend at least one meeting discussing and making these decisions. And expect to lose a few members who decide they aren't interested after all.

Who's in My Group?

✳

The sign-ups are in. Now you may have some choices to make.

What if you were planning only a small group, but got more sign-ups than anticipated? Rejoice! Be sure that everyone who signed up understands the commitment you expect and still wants to be in the group. Verify that they are qualified by whatever criteria you set. You may lose a few here who misunderstood or changed their minds. If the remaining number is still too large, see if you can find another leader and make two groups.

Now you're faced with the next decision. Who's in whose group? I suggest you don't take this issue lightly. I always like to meet with any other leaders to determine the groups. The book of Proverbs warns us, "Plans fail for lack of counsel, but with many advisers they succeed" (Proverbs 15:22). I usually don't know everyone who signs up for a study, and even if I do, the other leaders may know more or different details than I do. I can't tell you how often a discerning leader has prevented what might have been a tragic error in assignment by warning of personality conflicts or special needs. As we all work together, we have the combined wisdom to make these crucial decisions.

We begin with prayer. It's important to pray about the group divisions privately and with the other leaders before you begin the division. But I remember the time we failed to pray. What had in previous years been a 15-minute decision had already dragged on for almost an hour. Everyone wanted certain strong people in his or her groups. And no one wanted certain needy ones. We were deadlocked. Finally one of the leaders said, "You know, maybe we should pray about this."

Of course! In the frenzy of this meeting that we had squeezed into our already too busy schedules, we had jumped in without praying. No wonder we were having problems! We stopped and confessed our self-sufficiency and selfishness, then asked the Lord to decide. We went back to the list and had it divided within a few minutes.

And you know what? The divisions were perfect. As the year wore on, we could see why what each of us had wanted would never have worked. God knew what lay ahead for each person in the group. He knew who would suddenly move and who would have to drop out. He knew who needed special nurturing and who had a gift another especially needed. He knew what each of us would be able to handle by Christmas. And He was right.

When you assign people to groups there are some other matters to consider. Do you let prospective members choose their leader? While I'll certainly consider requests, I won't promise a specific leader or group. A lot depends on the reason for the request. I'll mention it to the leaders, but won't promise anything to the person making the request.

Do you put friends together? This is a tough one, and how you answer it may depend on the nature of the group. If one of the goals is to allow people to get to know more people in the church, you may want to avoid putting friends together. That will encourage each member to develop new relationships.

It may also depend on the nature of the friendship —and you may or may not know this. You may run the risk of a small clique within your group. Or you may find that, although a pair are very close, they'll be more open in a group away from their friend. On the other hand, one of the most dynamic groups I've ever led had three close friends in it. I actually went against my normal policy in allowing this, but I knew they really wanted to be together. I was apprehensive about a clique, but in this case it didn't develop. In fact, these friends reached out to new people and they each matured beautifully. Two are now in leadership in another group.

Do you divide based on needs or maturity? Do you put likes or unlikes together? It's always a good idea to have some mature people with some who are less mature, unless the study you're doing is geared specifically to mature Christians or to beginners. I've found that the less mature learn a lot from being with the more mature. And the enthusiasm of the young Christian recharges the more mature people.

"Only when each member makes a positive contribution does the group begin to achieve its potential. Each and every group member has an important contribution to make."
—Roberta Hestenes, *Using the Bible in Groups*

If you have more than one particularly needy person signing up, be sure to distribute them evenly! Most small groups can't effectively minister to more than one or two needy people, especially if the needs are multifaceted. And they always are.

Sometimes there's no question about where to meet. Most often, though, it's a decision you'll need to make. And it's a more important decision than you may realize. Your choices include churches, homes, offices, and other settings. But before we consider each of these, let's look at some general considerations.

First, how big is your group? A small group Bible study with six to ten members can meet almost anywhere. A larger ministry with 30 or more members is much more limited. You need to choose space large enough to accommodate everyone comfortably without being so large that people feel lost.

What kinds of space do you need? A small group may need only a room large enough to seat the group itself comfortably. A larger group will probably need both space for the whole group to meet and spaces for each small group. It's important, whenever possible, to provide each small group with a separate room, or at least with a well-defined, semi-private space to ensure confidentiality and to provide privacy for the laughter or tears that often are part of a small group.

Do you need tables? I always like to sit around a table. There's something homey about being able to see everyone, and it doesn't allow or force people to opt out of the group by sitting in an awkward location. It's helpful to have room to spread out my Bible, my study guide, and my coffee. It's so difficult to try to juggle everything on my lap, especially if I'm sitting on a folding chair. Even if you don't have a table everyone can sit around, it may help to provide some table space for Bibles and beverages.

Will you provide child care? You need to make this decision before choosing a meeting space. If you will include children, consider how many and what ages of children will need care.

Our church is young and full of children. I knew that we couldn't begin to think of a study for moms without including child care. I also knew that I needed

Considerations on Meeting Space

❋

"Jesus replied, 'Foxes have holes and birds of the air have nests, but the Son of Man has no place to lay his head'" (Matthew 8:20)

to plan on an average of two children per woman attending. When we started this ministry, we still didn't have our own church building. Finding a church large enough and willing to accommodate my estimates of 20 to 25 moms and 40 to 50 infants and preschoolers was an arduous task that I had to accomplish before we could even advertise the study.

What are the ages or special needs of your members? Small groups within our singles ministry could meet almost anywhere. Most of us were young and able to move around. Even a studio apartment with pillows on the floor worked fine. Upstairs or downstairs? It didn't matter. The same is not true for a group of older or handicapped adults. They may need firm straight chairs on the ground floor. Be sure to consider these needs before you commit to a space.

How far are people willing to travel when your study is scheduled? People have different ideas about travel. Be sure you understand those before you select a location.

Our singles ministry was in the heart of San Francisco and many members used public transportation. When we planned a small group, we needed to consider several factors. Was the site near a bus stop? How often did the buses stop at this location in the late evening? Was it a safe neighborhood for a single woman (or man!) to wait at night? How far away might you expect to park at night? Were there people with cars who lived near enough non-drivers to provide rides home? These considerations automatically eliminated some choices.

Now we live in the suburbs. When I finally found a church willing to host the Moms' Bible Study, it was a bit north of where most members of our church live. It would take most of them 15 minutes to drive there. I was thrilled to have found a meeting place, but I was astonished at the number of women who said that it was too far for them to drive. And the problem was actually their perception of the distance. The host church was three towns away, and it was perceived as a huge distance, even though it was only about five miles!

Many small group Bible studies meet in local churches. This is certainly the logical location for a large group that wants to begin together in worship, then break into small groups. It's also a wise choice if you plan to provide child care since that space will already be set up and large enough for your group.

Churches also usually have a supply of chairs and tables, so you can set up the rooms to support good group dynamics. They also often have a piano, organ, or other instruments that you can use for the worship time. And they probably have a large coffee pot. All you'll need to supply is someone to come early and start it!

Larger churches may have a janitorial staff that will set up for and clean up after all users. Most churches, however, don't have that luxury. As leader you'll need to add one more task to your job description—find someone to arrive early to set up and to stay afterward to clean up. Ideally this won't be yourself or your co-leader. This is an excellent opportunity to involve others in the ownership of the group, especially the shy or quiet members.

Be sure that you know how to adjust the heating and air conditioning, or get someone on staff to set the thermostat computer to come on a few hours before your group arrives. Nothing will hurt attendance like an uncomfortably hot or cold building, especially if parents are bringing their children.

Borrowing a Church Building

Increasingly churches meet in schools, theaters, community centers, and other public buildings rather than owning their own site. While these spaces work well for Sunday morning, they usually aren't available for mid-week ministries.

Does that mean if you don't have a church build-

Meeting in a Church Building

*

ing, you can't have a large Bible study ministry or provide child care? Of course not. It just means that it's a lot more work!

For years our women's ministries were limited to evening Bible studies that could fit in our church offices. As we grew, we squeezed out every other group that wanted space on Tuesday evenings, including staff and elders. We had small groups meeting everywhere except in the rest room—and don't think we hadn't considered that!

Then I got the bright idea of starting a Bible study for moms. Similar format, except in the morning and with child care. I should have checked into the nearest mental institution, but I believed this was the next step to which God was calling us. As I approached several potential leaders, the staff, and the elders, they agreed it was a need. But how could we handle it?

I spent countless hours that summer calling churches to find one that would lend or rent us space. It wasn't easy. Many of the large churches were already full every morning. And if they had space available, they were concerned about insurance and liability. Other churches were willing to have the women, but their child care space was too small for our young, growing church.

Finally we found a wonderful church that was delighted to have us. Their space was perfect for us, and their only requirement was that we put everything back the way we found it. We met at this generous, hospitable church rent free for two years.

In return we invited the staff to join us for refreshments during various social times. At Christmas we brought baskets of baked goods for the custodian. And at the end of each study year we asked the staff what large gift we could buy the church to show our appreciation. We felt that money, while always needed, would just get lost in the budget. Something tangible would remind them of our gratitude for years. Once we had their wish list, we'd decide how much money we needed to buy their gift and announce it for a couple of weeks. We always received more than enough.

If you need to borrow space, ask your staff, elders, and others at your church for names of acquaintances in other churches. A personal contact is priceless. Ultimately, this is what cinched it for us. I met the host church's minister's wife, and she went to bat for us.

When you make your request, be open to various options. We were willing to pay a reasonable rent, which we'd raise through offerings. We were also willing do our own set up and clean up. And we were flexible about which morning we'd meet. That made many church secretaries willing to at least take the request to the next level.

Work through or with the church secretary. Don't go behind her back or over her head. These women have a lot of influence and can make your task easier or more difficult. Chances are they'll be your contact while you are there, and they'll have a voice in renewing your agreement next year.

When you find a church willing to work with you, put your request in writing. That will help your contact clearly communicate your needs to the appropriate board or committee. It will also help to assure there are no surprises or loose ends that could get your relationship off on the wrong foot.

Treat the space as if it were your own. Encourage members to take personal responsibility to leave the building in better shape than you found it each week. Accommodate any idiosyncrasies of the staff. If they want chairs stacked upside down, stack them upside down. It's not your place to change their habits.

Don't take advantage of your host. If you say you'll be done by noon, be done by noon unless you make advance arrangements. If you use it, put it back. If you break it, fix or replace it.

Regularly remind your group how fortunate you are to have this space. Pray for your host church within the group.

Treat each year as a new request and a new agreement. Don't just assume that since you used it last year, you can use it this year. Staff change, boards change, ministries change. And after all, it is their property.

"The church facilities sometimes offer some things which a home cannot, such as nursery services for small children and ample parking. Also, persons are away from many of the things that can distract them from the group meeting, such as the telephone, children, and visitors who happen to stop by." —William Clemmons and Harvey Hester, *Growth Through Groups*

If your church finally moves into its own building, remember when you were aliens and strangers. Hold God's assets lightly; make them available to other groups.

Meeting in a Home

✳

Many small group Bible studies meet in homes. This is particularly true of a single small group. There's something inviting about meeting in a home. It's cozy. It's friendly. It's homey. And it may or may not be the best place for your group.

You need to consider the unique characteristics of your group and find a home that can best accommodate them. That may not be your home. Perhaps someone else's is larger, laid out better, or more centrally located. And perhaps someone else needs the opportunity to practice their gift of hospitality.

When you're deciding where to meet in a given home, consider the potential to create a comfortable atmosphere. Often you'll have more control over temperature and ventilation in a home than in a church or office. But sometimes temperature can be a problem. Many people keep their homes colder or warmer than the norm. And some don't have a lot of choice, especially as energy costs soar.

We heat with wood. Although we always try to bring the house to just the right temperature for a group, sometimes we fail. If we've been out all day it may take hours to warm the room. Or we'll have it perfect until half a dozen other warm bodies raise the temperature to just below sweltering.

Consider comfortable seating arrangements. When you meet in a home, you can often choose between sofas and chairs in a living or family room. Or you can meet around a table in the dining room or kitchen. See what the group's preferences are. If you use the living room or family room, be sure there are places for people to set beverages and Bibles.

Also be sure that the seating is comfortable. For the first several years we were married, my husband and I had two of the world's most uncomfortable sofas. One was low and soft, the other high and firm. Older visitors usually asked for straight chairs. Of course, we did find one advantage to these sofas. When we led the singles group at our church everyone arrived for meetings early because latecomers had to sit on the "deep dish sofa." To our surprise, meetings didn't last all night, either.

Check lighting levels. Even though we now have new sofas, our living room still has terrible lighting. It's fine for two of us, but the light isn't well distributed. For a group we supplement with lights taken from other parts of the house so our friends don't get eye strain as they read the fine print in their Bibles.

Keep distractions to a minimum. Distractions come in all shapes and sizes. Many are simply unavoidable, but others can be controlled. I know that people have different ideas about children and home Bible studies, and that even mentioning them will raise red flags for some readers. But please realize that not everyone feels as you do about children.

Unless otherwise agreed by the group, children need to be put to bed early or taught to remain quietly in their rooms during the group meeting. Otherwise, one parent should sit where he or she can get up inconspicuously and maintain order. Bible study evening is a good time for children to read books. It's not a good time for gangster movies on TV unless the children's rooms are far from the meeting area.

Try to meet in a home where the group isn't in the middle of common pathways. We don't have a family room. Our living room is between the kitchen and the bedrooms. If one of us has a group meeting everyone else is confined to the back part of the house. That doesn't seem fair, yet nothing will squelch honest disclosure faster than the fear that "As soon as I start talking, her husband will come strolling through." Even children passing through the room can put a damper on openness, so try to meet where you can reduce traffic distractions.

Noises from radios, televisions, and neighbors can also be distracting. Sometimes there's little you can do about the band practice of the teenagers next door, but if they're too distracting you may want to move the group to another location.

Of course, everyone's favorite distraction is the telephone! How often have you been in a home Bible study when the phone rang, the host answered it, and spent the next 45 minutes talking to someone totally unrelated to the study? For some reason we feel that if the phone rings we have to answer it.

The best alternative to answering the telephone is to let the answering machine get it. If the home you're in doesn't have a machine, turn off the ringer or put the phone under a pillow. Otherwise, by the time the caller gives up, the ringing will have driven everyone to distraction!

Parents often refuse to be out of touch with the baby-sitter. That's certainly reasonable. Give baby-sitters and others who may need to call a signal they can use. If you don't hear the signal, don't answer the phone. I'd do that even with a machine so the host won't need to get up and monitor the call.

Finally, consider that everyone may not love your pets as you do. I'm terribly allergic to cats. I'll never forget one small group we were in. It rotated between two homes so the families with children wouldn't have to hire sitters every week. One family had several long-haired cats that loved the living room. Often the cats were still inside when we arrived. No matter how well the hostess had vacuumed before we came or how cooperative they were in putting the cats out after we arrived, I'd sneeze from the minute I walked in the door until I left. Talk about distractions!

We don't have cats, but we did have a dog who loved to visit with guests. We still have a bird whose sole purpose in life is to sing. I don't even notice him anymore, but he may distract someone who isn't used to birds. Even if everyone loves your dog, when it's

"Christian small groups meet best in the homes of its members. Not only does this follow scriptural patterns, but it also has a lot of interpersonal advantages. Just by being in one's home, we come to know that person a lot better because the setting says a lot about the people who live there."
—Bob Parker, *Small Groups: Workable Wineskins*

time for the group to start, put him in another room.
And don't forget to cover the bird!

I guess the bottom line is that, while homes are
wonderful places to meet, we need to be sensitive to
concentration levels of the members. Some of us are
easily distracted. And anything that diverts attention
from worshiping, studying, sharing, or praying freely
must be addressed and resolved.

A Note About Zoning

Increasingly cities are using zoning ordinances to
limit home Bible studies and other religious activities
in residential neighborhoods. I'm not aware of any that
have been upheld in the courts, but it's worth checking
into before you invite a group to your home, especially
if that group will generate a lot of noise and/or traffic.

The argument used by the city fathers is that any
church activity in a home makes that home a church
building needing a permit. And since your home is not
zoned as a church, you can't sponsor church activities
there.

Although this is a serious infringement of our religious liberty, you need to decide if you're willing to
fight the battle. If your community has such restrictive
ordinances you can contact one of the Christian legal
organizations, such as the Rutherford Institute, Concerned Women for America, or the Western Center for
Law and Religious Freedom for advice.

Meeting in Other Settings

*

In addition to church buildings and homes, people
hold small group Bible studies in a variety of other
places. These include schools, restaurants, and parks,
as well as other private buildings available for meetings. Many of the considerations already described
will apply to these other places. In general, the fewer
distractions and the more privacy for sharing and

praying, the happier your group will be and the easier it will be for members to grow.

Many people like to have a Bible study during their lunch hour at work. An office or work setting is especially conducive to an evangelistic Bible study. Often businesses will provide conference rooms or allow employees to meet in their offices.

While you probably won't have the distractions of a home, you may have other equally disturbing diversions in an office. Some people will feel embarrassed attending a Bible study at work. Heaven forbid their bosses should catch them praying!

Try to get permission to use a space that won't have other demands on it. Can you schedule a conference room or other area that won't have a lot of traffic when you're meeting? Can you meet in your office, close the door, and turn off the phones?

Again, the more distractions you can reduce, the more open your group will be and the more the participants will grow toward maturity.

Checklist for Meeting Space
✳

Overall Considerations:

1) How big is your group?
   - Will you have more than one small group?
   - What is the maximum number of partici-pants you expect at any time?
2) What kinds of space do you need?
   - Do you need meeting space for a large group?
   - How many small group spaces do you need?
   - Do you need space for child care? If so, how many children, and what ages?
3) Seating
   - Do you need tables? If so, how many and how large? How many chairs or seats do you need?

- Do your potential members have any special needs, limitations, or other considerations (age, handicap, travel)?

If You Plan to Meet in a Church Building

1) Is your church facility available? Is it adequate for your needs?
2) Who will set up and clean up?
3) Who will arrive early to start the coffee and greet people?
4) Do you know how to adjust the room temperature controls?
5) Do you plan on borrowing or renting a church building? If so, do you know anyone to contact? Does anyone in your church have connections with members or staff in another church?
   - How much are you willing and able to pay for the space?
   - Are you willing to do your own set up and clean up?
   - What time and day do you need? How much flexibility do you have? Exactly how many hours do you expect to be in the space, including set up and clean up time?
   - If the church doesn't charge you rent, what will you do to thank them for their generosity?

If You Plan to Meet in a Home

1) Do you have more than one option for a host home? Consider the following for each option you have.
   - What are the obstacles to reaching the home at the time the study is scheduled? Consider traffic patterns, parking, bus routes, and safety.
   - How easily is the temperature controlled? Are there special considerations, like wood

"[Jesus] actually spent more time with His disciples than with everybody else in the world put together. He ate with them, slept with them, and talked with them for the most part of His entire active ministry. They walked together along the lonely roads; they visited together in the crowded cities; they sailed and fished together in the Sea of Galilee; they prayed together in the deserts and in the mountains; and they worshiped together in the synagogues and in the Temple."
—Robert E. Coleman, *The Master Plan of Evangelism*

stoves or radiant heating that take a long
time to warm a room? Is air conditioning
available if it's needed in your area?

- Is there adequate seating? Is it comfortable
for the types of people you plan to have in
the group?
- How is the lighting level at the time you plan
on having your study?
- What types of distractions are there? Can
they be reduced or removed?
- Are there children in the home whose noise
would cause a distraction?
- Is the layout of the home conducive to
privacy?
- Are there noisy neighbors?
- Are there pets? Is the owner willing to re-
move them from the room if they bother
members?
- Can you reasonably expect a zoning or other
legal problem? Would you expect com-
plaints from neighbors about either noise or
traffic?

If You Plan to Meet in an Office

1) Can you reserve a meeting space that has
little chance of being pre-empted by others?
2) What type of distractions or obstacles can
you expect? Can they be reduced?

If You Plan to Meet Elsewhere

1) Is the location convenient for everyone to
reach? Can you anticipate traffic, parking, or
other transportation problems?
2) Is there a reasonable amount of privacy? Is
there anything you can do to increase the
privacy or reduce the distractions?

Before your group begins—or at least within the first couple of weeks it meets—you need to decide whether your group will be open or closed. What does that mean?

An open group is like a Sunday-school class. It's open to new members at any time. People don't need to make a commitment. They just show up. Open groups may encourage regular attendance, but they really can't enforce attendance requirements.

It's essential that churches and parachurch organizations have some open groups to accommodate newcomers. People need a place to plug in immediately. Tell them that the next group will open in ten weeks and they'll probably look elsewhere.

In Careers, the interdenominational singles group in San Francisco, we had a wide variety of small groups, but the one you could always count on was the Thursday night Bible study. This open group required minimal commitment, and it was always there. Need a spiritual boost? Social life a little dead? Go to Thursday night Bible study. Someone will always be there. Year in and year out, it was the one group people could count on not to change. It was a great place to take new people. It helped them to feel like part of the group immediately. Lots of the "regulars" attended, so the sense of belonging came quickly.

Open groups, like Sunday school and Thursday night Bible study, can't incorporate all the elements of a small group. They often include both men and women, mature Christians and non-Christians, dedicated and not dedicated. Disclosure won't be as deep, and confidentiality may be a problem. But they're better than nothing. And they're essential to any large ministry.

Closed groups, by contrast, incorporate more of the essential elements we've discussed. They're a surefire path to maturity. But they're costly. They can

A Policy on Accepting New Members

✳

"I will make you fishers of men" (Matthew 4:19)

"Let us watch well our beginnings, and the results will manage themselves."
—Alexander Clark

consume people. Most people committed to other small groups weren't also part of Thursday night Bible Study. So a church or large ministry needs people committed to both types of groups.

Perhaps the most important thing you need to do in this regard is decide. Be clear about whether your group is open to new members, and if so, on what terms. Or is it closed, and if so, for how long? Is this negotiable? Under what conditions? People need to know this going in. You can't decide it after Joe has invited his cousin Rita to attend. You can't decide it when Jenny gets engaged. You need to agree in advance so there won't be any surprises or embarrassment.

Realize, however, that a closed group doesn't have to remain closed forever. I've been part of several groups that have had regular times of recommitment. This usually occurs after the first agreed-upon period is nearing completion.

For example, if you're doing a 13-week study, about the ninth or tenth week begin getting a sense of what people want to do next. Who wants to commit for another 13 weeks? Who wants (or needs) to move on? Give people a week or so to think and pray about their decision. Talk about it openly. Let people express their needs or preferences. Then decide if those who want to do it again want to open the group to new members. If so, how many? Who? What criteria will you use to decide?

I find that if the original group has been very close, about two-thirds of the members will continue while one-third will move on for various reasons. Expect the dynamics to change as new people join. I've rarely found the second group as close or as powerful as the first group, but there's no reason it can't be. It could be even better!

"If the purpose of the group includes building relationships of love and care among the members, a floating population will make it difficult, if not impossible, to accomplish the group's purpose."
—Roberta Hestenes, *Using the Bible in Groups*

Nothing will deflate a small group more quickly than disagreement about children. As the leader you may need to take a rather firm hand in this decision.

Let's consider two types of child care decisions. First, we'll look at an evening study where some or all of the participants have children. Then we'll consider providing child care during a study.

As much as we love children—and as much as we may subscribe to the idea of always keeping our children with us—we need to accept that having children around distracts many trying to understand a Bible passage or pray about a concern. And the resulting tension doesn't lend itself to happy children either.

Kids are wonderful. They're precious, and of course each of us feels that our children are the best behaved. But not everyone will agree—and we need to be open to that.

I really believe that the best policy is "no children." Some groups make an exception for nursing infants, but then find that the baby begins to be a distraction before the mother is ready to leave him home. That can cause a lot of frustration.

People want to be loving and considerate, but let's face it: some babies are a real distraction. It's hard to concentrate on a Bible study, prayer needs, or prayer with junior wailing in the background or crawling around chewing everyone's toes. Then you run into ill feelings from other parents who've paid a sitter and were expecting a pleasant evening out.

It's always better to discuss such policies in the beginning while they're still abstract. That also allows parents to decide if they can commit to being a part of the group or not. And it's a lot easier to agree that we'll allow nursing babies up to three months of age rather than having to tell Barbara and Ken that their five-month-old is becoming a distraction.

The discussion of meeting places mentioned noise

A Policy on Children

✻

"Let the little children come to me" (Mark 10:14)

from host children. This can be a serious problem. Some people have the concentration of a juggler. The house has to be in danger of demolition before they notice the joyful screams of their little dears. Others, particularly those without children, will notice and be distracted by every sound. Both of these extremes are probably unhealthy, but believe me, if there are children around, you'll have at least one of each in your group.

If possible, meet in a location without children. If that's not possible, try to choose a home where the children's area is far away from the meeting area. Lacking that, you'll want to discuss the issue frankly before it becomes a problem.

Using a baby-sitter is often a problem for many Christian parents. Some have philosophical objections to leaving their children with others, and some simply can't afford it. One solution many people in our church's community groups use is to trade sitting with friends. Someone in a Tuesday night group cares for the children of their friends in a Wednesday night group, then they swap on Wednesday. It's cheap and gives the children a chance to be with their friends, but it does require a commitment of two nights per week from each family.

I've always thought it would be a wonderful ministry for the high school group or senior citizens to provide free in-home care for parents who can't afford a weekly baby-sitter. Of course, I've never seen this happen, but what if . . . ?

Should You Provide Child Care?

✳

In my mind, this question is second only to, "Should I jump out of an eight story building?" I've led a study that provided child care, and yes, I'm sure I'll do it again. But it's a much bigger task than you may have bargained for.

When we decided to start the Moms' Bible Study, our first decision was that we wouldn't proceed without paid, quality child care. I based this decision on experience and it was a good one. It's just that it was far more difficult to pull off than anyone anticipated.

Years ago our church had a Bible study for moms. The members provided child care on a rotation basis. We signed up in advance for "our weeks." The problem wasn't the moms. It was the children. They kept getting sick! So every week it seemed that two of the three moms scheduled to work had sick children and didn't come. Others had to fill in. Since it was a small group anyway, it was easy to miss three out of four weeks of the study. By then, why bother even coming? Those women had lost the continuity of both the study and the prayer needs. They were burned out. If they had wanted to take care of children, they'd have stayed home! And they did. Soon the study just petered out.

So we knew that a successful moms' study would need consistent, high quality, paid child care by people who had no delusions of attending the study. Since our church has many women with two or more preschoolers, often very close together, we wanted to give them a break. We also wanted the time to be more than baby-sitting for the children by providing a quality program for the preschoolers.

I was fortunate to find a mother who agreed to co-ordinate child care. "Nothing to it!" we thought. We began looking for workers in mid-summer. We made it a matter of regular prayer among the leadership. But when the study began in late September, we had only three care givers. We needed at least four. After several months, we did find four women who were willing to work, but we never had back-ups.

We thought we'd find grandmothers, women from other churches, or mothers who wanted to earn some extra money. What we learned was that, at least in our area, there just aren't many women at home who want to serve in a child care ministry—even a paid one! We called every church in the area. Our request was usually met with, "If you find anyone, give them our phone number." Older women are working or enjoying their retirement. Younger women are working or are busy with other activities.

The three factors that finally contributed to our finding the workers we needed were prayer, prayer, and prayer. It took a while, but soon the entire group had made our need a matter of regular prayer, as well as regular searching.

Each year it has become progressively more difficult to provide child care. One year two Bible study leaders began the year working in the nursery. (It's easier to get leaders than to get child care workers!) And each year, at least one of the workers has brought her own children, adding to the workload while providing much-needed care.

Is it worth it? Even after all the effort, I'd have to say yes. It's difficult to get good care. But you simply can't provide a daytime Bible study for mothers without it.

Every church I'm familiar with in our area has had the same experience. Some provide child care for evening groups and classes at the church. It's still difficult to coordinate, but at least in the evening they have teenagers available.

If I haven't discouraged you from providing child care, let's look at some keys to success.

Plan on Paying

There seems to be an expectation today that child care, even in the church, is a job, not a ministry. Gone are the grandmothers with the time and interest in

"If group members have children, then arrangements need to be made for them. Sensitivity needs to be shown here, especially towards young mothers who are often expected to care for children rather than participate fully in the group without fear of distraction. Unless the group is a family group designed to include children in its activities, arrangements should be made for children to be

helping out young mothers. Today many grandmothers are young and active. Many are working outside the home, often beginning a second career. But even among those who don't have jobs, few are available for child care. Several claimed that they'd cared for their own children for years; now they were due for a rest. Also, the men and women of any age who have a heart for children are usually consumed in the Sunday school program, Awana, Boys' Brigade, Pioneer Clubs, Good News Clubs, and other children's programs. There are more than enough places to serve these days.

So from the beginning we planned to pay a reasonable wage. We paid a flat fee for the morning. Although our rate was more than fair, we weren't swamped with takers. We also learned that if you expect the worker to teach a lesson, the rate goes up.

If you don't have a budget from your church, you should be able to cover the costs through offerings. The cost per mom is certainly less than each would have to pay individually—assuming she could even find daytime care. We found that those who could pay more always covered those who couldn't pay much. It's essential, however, to guarantee the rate to your workers regardless of your budget or income. That may mean that your leaders or someone else needs to commit to making up any shortfall.

Maintain A Reasonable Ratio

Our goal was one worker per four babies and toddlers and one worker per six preschoolers (ages 2 to 5). We didn't always make it, but that was what we based our budget on, and that's what we continued to seek.

If your child-to-worker ratio is too high, parents will be uncomfortable and simply won't attend. Mothers must be certain that their children are being well cared for before they can relax and enjoy the study.

If your numbers, workers, and space permit it, divide the preschoolers into one group of 2's and 3's and another of 4's and 5's. The developmental difference between two and five is tremendous. It's tough

cared for away from the group meeting room. A baby-sitter can be arranged or couples can take turns being responsible for the children. It might be that the cost of a baby-sitter could be shared by the whole group."
—Roberta Hestenes, *Using the Bible in Groups*

to plan activities that will maintain the interest of such a wide age spread.

Treat Your Workers With Consideration

You know that your workers are valuable to your ministry. Let them know that! We always take a special offering to buy gifts for them at Christmas and at the end of the year. During our Christmas and end-of-the-year parties, we have moms trade off working with the children so the workers can join the celebration.

Even more important than gifts is your willingness to honor your time commitments to them, especially if you're paying a flat fee. If your study is to end at 11:00, end it at 11:00! Children must have built-in clocks! They know when their moms should pick them up. If your group is late the children can become difficult for the best teacher—and at the time she's the most tired.

Be clear in the beginning just what you expect from the workers in each area. We expected them to arrive 30 minutes before the study began. This allowed them to care for the leaders' children while we met for prayer. It also gave them a chance to set up each room as they wanted it. That way, by the time most of the children arrived, they were prepared.

We also expected them to remain for 30 minutes after the study ended. This allowed plenty of time to get the room cleaned up. Of course, if they finished early, they were free to leave. Several moms often stayed and helped them clean up. That was just another way of saying, "Thanks! We love you!"

We also expected the workers in the preschool room to plan a story, a simple lesson, and a craft. While the children had adequate time for free play, we didn't want the time to be little more than supervised chaos. We wanted to introduce the children to Jesus and encourage them to love Him more. For many, Tuesday morning became a highlight of the week.

"If I were asked what single qualification was necessary for one who has the care of children, I should say patience—patience with their tempers, with their understandings, with their progress."
—Francis de S. Fenelon

Try to Hire Christians

When we began the child care program, we naturally assumed that the workers would be Christian. As time went on and we had no one, we decided to re-evaluate this criterion. We decided that since the infants and toddlers were not going to be taught a lesson, any loving person who was good with children could care for them. We monitored them carefully, but felt some freedom here.

We were insistent, however, that those caring for the preschoolers had to be Christians. This was a difficult decision. After weeks of being short-handed, we were tempted to take anyone still breathing! But we were convinced that the Lord would not have us subject our children to false or inadequate teaching simply so the moms could enjoy a Bible study.

You may decide on a different policy, particularly if you don't plan on having the workers teach a lesson. But I would encourage you to make your decision carefully and prayerfully, then stick to it.

CHAPTER 6

Hey! I'm a Leader!

WE'VE COVERED A lot of preliminaries. By now, you're ready to begin your small group Bible study. We'll spend the first part of this chapter preparing for that all-important first meeting, and the second part introducing the fundamentals of managing the group.

First impressions are important. As the old saying goes, "You only have one chance to make a first impression." I can't emphasize enough the importance of your group's first meeting. The impressions created there will almost certainly influence how your group functions for weeks or even months to come.

If you're uneasy, unprepared, or thoughtless, your group will feel it and will respond accordingly. Likewise, if you're comfortable, prepared, and thoughtful, your group will respond as you had hoped.

"There is a time for everything, and a season for every activity under heaven" (Ecclesiastes 3:1)

Expect some discomfort or uneasiness among members of your group during the first couple of meetings. Even if everyone knows one another, if they haven't all been part of the same group before, they're facing an unknown. And few of us like unknowns. We face them with apprehension.

What will people be thinking as they come to the first meeting? They'll wonder who you are and why you're the leader. They'll wonder who these other people are and if they'll like them—and what to do if they don't. They'll wonder how much of themselves they'll need to reveal. They'll wonder if they will like the study. They'll wonder if it will take too much time. Notice that most new members will focus on the threats rather than on the opportunities.

Understand the Life Cycle of Small Groups

✳

As the leader it's your job to recognize their probable uneasiness and do all you can to reduce it. One of the first ways to do this is to recognize that small groups, like every other organism, have a predictable life cycle. Understanding this life cycle will help you understand what to expect from your group. It will also help you prepare for the first meeting.

Early in the life of the group, the leader must take most of the initiative to reduce the discomfort of the members. The newcomer, not wanting to invest much in a group he may not like, often sits back and watches. This can be a perplexing time for the new leader, especially if he doesn't understand group life cycles.

A good leader will begin immediately to build ownership among the members of the group. But he'll also realize that it won't come instantly. The members will want to become comfortable and decide they're staying before getting too involved. The leader must create a climate that allows the members to become integrated within the first few meetings.

Once he's achieved this integration, usually in three or four weeks, the leader can relax a bit, at least in the amount of initiative he must show. Others will begin to take some responsibility for the group. Soon it will truly be "our" group rather than merely "your" group. More members will begin to take responsibility in different ways, whether that is in encouraging, suggesting, telephoning, or serving.

Finally, as the predetermined time for the end of the group draws near, the leader must again exert more responsibility and initiative. The group needs to decide if they're going to continue, end, or resume after a break. They need to decide if they'll invite new people to form a new group. There needs to be closure, especially for those not continuing. There needs to be a symbolic ending of the group. While everyone will be involved in these decisions, the leader needs to make sure that they happen in a positive way.

Understanding the life cycle of groups will give you confidence as you face your group for the first time. Let's look at some additional ways you can create a welcoming atmosphere for your group.

> "Group unity and participation are encouraged as leadership flows from person to person, with the designated leader making sure that it happens."—A Small Group, *Good Things Come in Small Groups*

Prepare With Prayer

✳

> "Very early in the morning, while it was still dark, Jesus got up, left the house and went off to a solitary place, where he prayed" (Mark 1:35)

I hope you've been preparing for the group by praying about every detail as you've faced it. And I hope you've prayed a great deal about the particulars of this first meeting. Now is a good time to institute a tradition that will serve both you and your group well. I hope you'll consider it also.

Anytime I lead a small group, I ask the leaders and co-leaders to commit themselves to arrive 30 minutes before the group is to begin. This commitment is not only for the first meeting, but also for every meeting of the group. And it's part of their overall commitment. If a person can't agree to come early, it's unlikely that I'll be able to use him or her in the leadership of this study.

Why so early? There are several reasons. I want the leaders to have a chance to slow down, focus their thinking on the group, deal with any questions they might have, and most of all, pray. Let's look at these needs.

First, you don't want your leaders rushing in along with everyone else. You want them to be there early, prepared to greet the members calmly. You want them to have a few extra minutes in case they're caught in traffic. You want them to have switched gears mentally before the group arrives so they can minister to those who are late and frazzled. That takes time. There's no way around it. Insist that they commit to that extra 30 minutes.

Second, you want to give them time to resolve any questions they might have on the lesson. Perhaps one didn't understand a question and wants clarification from the others. Perhaps another needs an example to use as an object lesson or a good opening question. Perhaps still another has the perfect illustration that the rest of you can use. Take part of the 30 minutes to deal with such issues.

Finally, you need time to invite the Lord to be present with you. You need to seek Him in prayer. You need to be refreshed by His presence. And you may need to pray for a leader or co-leader who's hurting so he or she can be free to minister to the rest of the group. Spend at least half of the 30 minutes in prayer.

You'll find that as time goes on, leaders and co-leaders will begin to arrive later and later. They'll always have good excuses, and they are trying, so you don't want to come down too hard on them. But I can assure you that if you wait for everyone to arrive and if you don't insist on promptness, you won't have time for prayer. Within a short time your leadership meeting will begin 10 minutes before the study rather than 30 minutes before. So keep your leaders faithful to their commitment to this time.

What if your study is only one small group and you don't have a co-leader? Shame on you! Review the information on co-leaders in Chapter 5 and see if you have a good reason for not having one. Then, regardless of your decision, plan on devoting the 30 minutes

"I believe that we get an answer to our prayers when we are willing to obey what is implicit in that answer. I believe that we get a vision of God when we are willing to accept what that vision does to us."
—Elsie Chamberlain

"Do you know what is wrong with the world today? There's too much theologian and not enough kneeologian."
—Dallas F. Billington, *Akron Baptist Journal*

before the study to personal preparation and prayer. Consider that your commitment actually begins 30 minutes before the starting time of the group. Go over any announcements you need to make. Be sure you have the handouts you need. Think through any questions that you need to address. Pray and allow the Lord to refresh you. Then go out in His strength and minister to your group.

Make People Feel Prepared For

✳

"Practice hospitality" (Romans 12:13)

One of the first things you can do to reduce uneasiness is to create a relaxed and welcoming atmosphere, which can only come from thoughtful preparation. This will show that you've considered what the members will be feeling and that you care about easing their tension.

Look over your meeting space. Check tables, seating arrangements, lighting, ventilation, and distractions. Deal with any problems in advance if you can. And be sure to have the meeting space set up before people arrive. Nothing makes so poor an impression than waiting until people walk in to begin gathering chairs. Work with your co-leader, host or hostess, or someone else in the group if necessary, but have the room set up the way you want it. Then consider some additional elements to welcome your group.

See the sections in Chapter 5 on meeting space for details.

Your First Meeting

The first meeting is full of announcements and instructions. You'll find that you're doing a lot of talking. You'll want to find ways of involving others as much as possible while still covering all you need to this first time together.

Your first item of business is to make sure everyone knows who you and any other leaders are. Begin by introducing yourself. Tell what's important for them to know about you, then ask the other leaders to do the same. This usually includes name, family, and a one-

or two-minute testimony of how and when you became a Christian.

After introductions, clearly state your goal for the group. Why are you leading or why did you start this group? What do you hope to see accomplished in the members' lives by the end of your time together? This is a good time to share your vision or goals for the first time.

After talking about your goals for the group, stress the need for members to commit themselves to attend regularly and to prepare for each meeting. Don't skip this vital step. Don't assume that everyone understands it, even if you've personally discussed it with each. They need to hear it in the group setting to expect it in the group setting.

If you're going to allow the group to set attendance and preparation requirements tell them that you will, but put off discussion until the next meeting when people are a little more comfortable with one another. I'd suggest several alternatives and ask people to think and pray about them, then come prepared to make a decision at the next meeting.

Next discuss the ground rules for the small group(s). Include in this discussion the need for honest disclosure, accountability, confidentiality, and commitment to growth or maturity. Next mention any special rules on space, finances, child care, time, and such. This lets people know up front exactly what is expected of them. This is also a good time to discuss details like refreshments. Again, if the group is going to decide, give members the options for discussion at the next meeting.

These introductions will take at least 15 minutes, perhaps as long as 20 or 25 minutes if it's a large group with lots of details. When you finish them is a good time to change gears with a time of worship.

Since you've been doing most of the talking, consider having someone else lead in this time. Maybe it will be the person you've asked to lead worship regularly. Maybe it will be your co-leader. But try to give someone else the spotlight now. Take some time for worship. Include group singing and a special reading, some Scripture, or whatever you think the group will be most comfortable with. Today is not the time to introduce a new form of worship.

Following the worship you may wish to take a few minutes to introduce the study. Ideally people already have their study guides and will have read the introduction. If not, you'll want to take time to address that briefly. Discuss the purpose, content, and expected results of this particular study. Mention why you selected it.

Finally, spend some time in your small group(s) getting to know one another. This is a good time to use one or more get-acquainted opening questions, depending on your time. Appendix C presents several of these. Allow people to share as much or as little as they're comfortable with. Don't probe or prod this time. Let people get used to hearing the sounds of their voices in this room with this group of people. Let them take some time to develop trust of and love for one another. For some people, even introducing themselves in a group can be traumatic.

It may encourage you to know that, regardless of how the group was formed or who is in it, it's been my experience that people in the group almost always are comfortable with one another by the third meeting. I've lost track of the times people have said, "When this group began, I wasn't sure I'd like it. Now I can't imagine being in any other group!" If you've left the membership decisions to God, He'll amaze you with the results!

Should You Serve Refreshments?

There rages today a major controversy over refreshments in small groups. One side says that refreshments are essential. The other says they're a waste of time, and that, with people's busy schedules, no one wants one more detail to be responsible for. Then they add that, considering the widespread problem of obesity, who needs more calories?

I happen to be on the side of the "essential." Have you ever noticed that when Christians gather they tend to eat? Who has better potlucks than Christians?

But the food isn't an end in itself. Rather, it's a means to an end—the goal of fellowship and community. Somehow, having a cup or cookie to hold onto creates an illusion of confidence. People are friendlier, more willing to slow down and talk with one another. Food also says, "You're welcome here." The aroma of coffee or cinnamon tea brewing and some light refreshments say, "I've taken time to prepare for you. You're important." That's why I consider refreshments an essential for the first meeting of any small group.

You want people to feel prepared for. You want them to know that they're important to you. You want them to know that this group wasn't an afterthought. And since you're being considerate, be sensitive to those on low-fat and low-cholesterol diets. Personally, I think we ought to have brownies every week, but fruit or low-calorie desserts will be appreciated by many.

As a group you may later decide to eliminate or limit refreshments. But please, for the first meeting or two, take the responsibility to prepare for your group.

Another welcoming touch, especially for the first meeting, is a centerpiece or other "room warmer." Especially if you're meeting in a cold, sterile fellowship hall or Sunday-school room, a centerpiece adds a warmth that's hard to match. Even in a home it communicates caring. Your centerpiece doesn't need to be fresh flowers. It can be almost anything. I've used a pumpkin and some autumn leaves on a woven place mat. I've used interesting cookie jars, pottery, or potted plants. I've used a quilt to cover a table. A male friend uses a huge basket of sea shells on his table. Anything that adds a bit of color and interest will go a long way in helping people feel at home during their first meeting. You're creating a first impression of care and concern.

Rather than feeling that you need to heap the responsibility for refreshments and the table setting on yourself, seek a couple of people who will coordinate

"Remember especially during this first meeting that you will be getting together each week for a group discussion. You are the leader—not the director. Be unpretentious and honest. Don't put on airs of superiority, but exhibit the quiet confidence that comes from having a plan to serve the other group members, and knowing how to execute it." —NavPress, *How to Lead Small Group Bible Studies*

these areas. Again, this helps to create ownership in the group as more people take on responsibility. And it's a great training ground for leadership. Remember what Jesus said in the parable of the talents: "You have been faithful with a few things; I will put you in charge of many things" (Matthew 25:23).

Honoring Time Commitments

Before the group began you probably decided how many weeks it would run or decided that it would continue indefinitely. That's an important timing decision to communicate to the group during your first meeting.

There's another important timing decision that should begin at the first meeting and continue for every meeting thereafter. That is, you must start on time and you must stop on time. If you don't honor this time commitment, your group will quickly become unwieldy and people will lose interest.

It's essential that you agree on a starting time, then start at that time regardless of who is or isn't present. If you wait until everyone has arrived you'll soon find that the starting time moves five minutes later each week. Before long, people will know that your 7:30 meeting really means it'll start at 7:50. They won't show up until 7:45. Then you'll need to continue later into the evening or cut something short. That's not the way to honor your commitment to your group or to encourage them to honor their commitment to one another. Agree on a starting time and start at that time.

It's also important for the meeting to end when you say it will. People plan their schedules according to when they expect the group to begin and end. If you consistently allow the group to run beyond the agreed-upon ending time, you'll find that people are unhappy. Set a time limit for each portion of the meeting (worship, discussion, disclosure, and prayer). Do your best to follow that schedule. Regardless, end on time.

If you have refreshments, it often works well to serve them at the end of the study. That way if people need to leave they can do so. Those who aren't in a

"The role of the leader . . . is to be sensitive to process and to individuals. He designs various experiences that the group can share so that each individual can grow personally and contribute to the growth of others."
—Lawrence Richards and Gib Martin, *A Theology of Personal Ministry*

hurry can stay and visit. The exceptions to this might be a morning study or one that meets over lunch, when you'll want to serve during the meeting.

Keys to Leading a Good Discussion

✳

"Do your best to present yourself to God as one approved, a workman who does not need to be ashamed and who correctly handles the word of truth" (2 Timothy 2:15)

Remember that in this type of small group, you're not the teacher, but merely a facilitator. That in itself relieves you of a huge responsibility. No one expects you to have all the answers nor to do all the talking. In fact, if you do, you'll seriously compromise the group approach!

Webster's New Collegiate Dictionary defines "facilitate" as, "to make easier." That's simple enough. Your job as the facilitator is to make it easier for the members of your group to understand Scripture, to discuss their findings, and to apply it to their lives.

First, let's understand that the goal of the discussion is to allow the group members to share what they've learned from their own personal study of God's Word. As they interact with one another, their own understanding will be enhanced and expanded. They will gain new insights. And the results will be far greater than if you had simply taught, or fed them, the lesson based on your understanding and insights.

In leading the discussion, you'll want to put together all you've learned in this book. And you'll want to understand group dynamics so you can encourage each member to come away from the discussion with more than he brought to it. You'll do this primarily through the vehicles of asking questions and encouraging application.

Let's look at a few simple rules of facilitating, or making the discussion flow smoothly.

Don't Monopolize

If your goal is to make it easier for members of your group to understand God's Word, you need to let them talk. By definition, that means you do less talking and they do more talking.

That's not as easy as it sounds. As the leader you will probably be better prepared than most members of the group. You'll have gained wonderful insights. It's hard to stop yourself from sharing them. Just realize that the more you talk the less they will talk.

"But who can keep from speaking?" Job 4:2).

And that's not just because they won't have time. They'll actually be demotivated. They'll lose their interest in sharing. They'll assume they don't have anything important to say. And pretty soon they'll even stop doing their lessons. Then the burden will fall on you, and before you know it you'll be teaching rather than facilitating!

Make sure that you talk, even in asking questions, less than your "share" of the time. That means that if your eight-member group has 48 minutes to discuss the lesson, you should be talking less than six minutes. You won't want to be so obvious as to use a stop watch, but pay attention to who is doing most of the talking. If it's you, then you need to find a new way to lead.

For additional tips on mono- polizers and getting others to talk, be sure to read Chapter 7, "Why Didn't You Warn Me?"

Listen Actively

It seems almost contradictory to say that a facilita- tor must be a listener. You'd think that a facilitator should be a talker, wouldn't you? Actually, you'll stimulate much better learning by listening to your group members than by talking to them. There are several keys to listening that will cause your group members to rise up and call you blessed.

When listening, use your whole body, not just your ears. Practice good body language. This means you need to show by your posture and responses that you're paying full attention to what each person says.

Look each speaker in the eye. Make eye contact. Lean forward just a bit. Nod in agreement or under- standing. Allow your face to express the emotions you're feeling. This technique is called attending.

Pay attention. Show enthusiasm for the material

"If you would be pungent, be brief; for it is with words as with sunbeams—the more they are condensed, the deeper they burn." —Robert Southey

and for your members' responses. Move the respondent beyond obvious or cliché answers by probing a bit deeper. Ask, "Can you explain how you were blessed?" or, "Tell us how you felt when you came to that new understanding."

Move the respondent to greater personal understanding by making open-ended statements like, "It sounds as if you really gained a new appreciation for forgiveness in this lesson," or "That new realization must have caused you some pain." Such active listening helps the speaker gain an even clearer grasp of his or her own thought process.

As you listen to your members' responses be alert for judgmental replies, legalisms, pat answers, and other discussion-enders. Use active listening techniques to draw the person out of the comfort zone of his response. Encourage other members to respond not only to the original question, but also to one another's responses. Your task through all of this is to maintain order and a spirit of cooperative learning. You'll also need to guard yourself so you aren't the one with the judgmental or legalistic responses.

Be sure to reread "Nurturing Transparency" in Chapter 3 to review the core conditions of empathy, warmth, and respect.

Here's an important key: people remember best that which they have said themselves and have applied experientially. As the facilitator, help your members to express themselves clearly and cogently. They will remember the lesson much longer than if you simply rephrase their response or answer the question for them.

Finally, as a facilitator, you need to maintain a balance in your attitude. On one hand you need to be gentle and gracious. Never say or do anything that will offend or hurt a group member. At the same time, however, you must be tough and directive. Keep the discussion moving in the direction you planned it to go. Don't let people get away with being shallow or rude, and don't let them go off on tangents.

As a leader it's essential that you take your responsibility seriously. Take sufficient time to prepare to lead the discussion. First do the assignment everyone else is doing. Then go beyond the assignment.

Use the leaders' guide if one is available with your study. This will often give you additional biblical or cultural information that you can pass on to your group. If a leaders' guide is not part of the study, you'll need to dig deeper on your own. Appendix A will introduce you to some helpful study resources.

As you prepare, use your time efficiently. You can't research every interesting question and follow every rabbit trail. Biographical or archeological information may be interesting, but is it useful to the discussion you want to lead? Consider your group. What do the members need to take away from this lesson? What are the two or three most important ideas in it? Focus your study on these.

Preparing to Lead the Discussion

*

"The sluggard craves and gets nothing, but the desires of the diligent are fully satisfied" (Proverbs 13:4)

Use a Lesson Plan

I like to use a lesson plan form to help organize my thoughts for leading the discussion. I've included a blank lesson plan form in Appendix D.

Before you begin your next study, reproduce enough copies of the lesson plan form to use one with each lesson. (You may want to retype it on 8 1/2" by 11" paper to make it easier to work with.) Then they'll be ready for you for the duration of the group.

After you've considered what one or two ideas are most important from each lesson, summarize these main points on the "summary" lines of the lesson plan. An excellent way to do this is to write your summary in principle form. A principle is a short statement of the main point of the lesson. It's never more than a sentence or two, and it often contains a memorable phrase to plant the lesson firmly in the mind and heart.

Following the summary or principle, develop one or more goals or behavioral objectives. Exactly what is it you want people to come away with? How do you want them to change their behavior, thoughts, attitudes, or beliefs based on this lesson? State this in terms of how you expect people to apply the lesson.

As I'm leading the lesson, these two elements—the summary and the goal—guide me. They light my path and keep me on track. And hopefully if I stay on track, so will the rest of the group.

You need to know that what you see as the main point of the lesson may be very different from what I see as the main point. Usually this doesn't mean one of us is wrong. Rather, we've selected different points that apply most closely to ourselves and our group members. Most study guide lessons are written broadly enough that you can select from several threads. As long as you're sure that the thread you've selected is biblically sound, go for it!

Plan Your Questions

Realize in advance that you can't discuss every question in the study guide during your group discussion. There simply isn't enough time. Therefore you'll need to select a few pertinent questions that advance your goal. You may even want to write your own questions or combine two or more from the study guide to move in the direction of your goal.

"Success is 10 percent inspiration and 90 percent perspiration."
—Thomas Edison

Since we won't have time to discuss every question, I make it clear to my groups that I expect them to have done their homework. I also expect them to understand the objective questions unless they ask for clarification. Then we seldom discuss an objective question. There's no point in using our limited time parroting "right answers." But if the members haven't done those, they'll have no idea what we're talking about.

Rather than trying to find my way through the study guide while concentrating on the discussion, I again like to use the lesson plan. I select or develop five to seven key questions—some interpretation and some application—and list those on the lesson plan. In leading a discussion I prefer to focus on interpretation and application, since I'm convinced that's where growth occurs best. It's also easiest to get into a great discussion using these types of questions.

Answering an observation question is pretty boring —the response is so obvious! Interpretation and application questions usually have less obvious answers and allow more give and take. They even allow disagreement, and that's OK. Don't be afraid of friendly disagreement. Remember, the more the members of your group are talking, the less you'll need to do. However, there is one way that interpretation and application questions can be as lethal to a discussion as observation questions. That's if you ask the question in such a way that it predetermines the answer. Boring!

This may be a fault of the study guide. Or it may be you've found only one possible response, so you phrase your question to trigger that answer. Either way you're reducing your chances for encouraging a good discussion.

Even if a group member comes up with the obvious answer, take time to probe and see if anyone else had a different response. That will generate discussion. Note that if a question can be answered with a yes or no, it's probably obvious.

Types of Discussion Questions

✳

"Do not merely listen to the word, and so deceive yourselves. Do what it says" (James 1:22)

Regardless of whether or not your study guide provides you with good questions, your responsibility as a facilitator is to ask good questions. And those questions should always move you in the direction of the goal you set previously.

There are three general types of questions that you should ask, and an additional type you may want to ask.

Launching questions, sometimes also called approach questions, point the direction of the discussion. They communicate to your group members which of several possible directions you've decided to pursue. A launching question is anything that will open the discussion. A good launching question may or may not be in the study guide. If a study guide has an ice-breaker question, that may be a good launching question if it points in the direction you've decided to go. If it doesn't advance that goal, don't use it. Make up your own. Or you may find a good launching question elsewhere in the text of the lesson.

As you select a launching question it's important to sense the mood, the skill or knowledge level, and the openness of the group members with one another. Hopefully all of these will change as the group progresses. As they do, your launching questions will also need to change. You may find that the icebreaker question is great as your group begins, but within a few weeks it's too shallow.

When your group is beginning, don't go too deep too fast, but also avoid starting at such a shallow level that it doesn't provide a challenge. I always try to stay just one step ahead of my group's comfort zone. That way I'm always stretching them to go deeper and to get more serious about their walk with the Lord and with one another.

Guiding questions are just what the name implies. They continue the discussion in the direction you've chosen. They keep the discussion moving toward the goal.

Guiding questions tend to build on each other. Each question logically and naturally leads to the next. By having already selected your guiding questions it's easier to avoid digressions or "rabbit trails." This is particularly important if you have someone in your group who excels in tangents!

By definition guiding questions eliminate some discussion directions that you didn't choose. That will usually be OK with your group members, but what if it isn't? What if, directly or indirectly, one or more members decide to pursue a different direction?

At this point you need to make a judgment call. I may lay the choice before the group, or I may simply

decide to continue in the direction I've planned. If I
feel my goal is getting away from me, it's easy enough
to say something like, "Terry brings up an interesting
point. I wish we had time to pursue it. However, in
studying this passage, I felt that the most pertinent
issue for our group to discuss was the way Joshua
confronted his fear. Let's address that now. Then if we
have time, we can come back and talk about the
historical issues. OK?"

Probably no one will object, unless your interpretation of the most important lesson is way off. In fact,
they may be impressed that you're so well prepared
that you can articulate the issues! Of course, if enough
people want to move in another direction, you may
need to wing it.

If you find that your group is particularly interested
in the historical or cultural background, you might
consider devoting five minutes to that at the beginning
of the study. Or you may want to put together a one-
page background sheet that members can read at their
leisure. This will honor their interest, and at the same
time allow you to focus on the more application-
oriented aspects of the study.

Note that the lesson plan form provides for three
sections, or sets, of guiding questions. In some lessons
you'll want to explore more than one direction. In
other lessons one direction will be more than enough.
Adapt the format to serve you.

Summary and application pull the study together
and put it to work. They summarize in a practical,
attainable way what the group has learned.

Ideally you've used several application questions
throughout the discussion. I always strive to keep any
Bible study discussion as application-oriented as possible. If I don't it's simply too easy for the group—and
for me—to make it into a heady, academic study. My
attitude as I lead the discussion is always, "So what?
What can I do with this information today, in my life,
right where I am?"

If you've followed this principle throughout the
discussion, you've already been talking about

application. Even so, it's important to save enough time near the end of the discussion to first summarize, and then apply. In developing your lesson plan, complete the conclusion section, including the segments for summary and application. As the discussion progresses make a few notes in that section. If Carol makes a particularly good point related to the summary, note it. If Jack suggested a new insight on how he'll apply it, note that. Then when you reach the summary and application stage you'll be able to retrieve those comments. Members will be pleased that you remembered something they said and that you considered it important enough to note!

"God save us from hotheads who would lead us foolishly, and from cold feet that would keep us from adventuring at all."
—Peter Marshall

The summary and application can be a question, a statement, or both. You may say, "OK, let's summarize. We've seen that first, Joshua trusted the Lord even when he couldn't see the outcome. And second, we've seen that God said the key to Joshua's success would be to meditate on God's Word, then do it. Let's think for a minute. What one action can you take this week to conquer the fear you feel surrounding your personal giant?"

Give the group a minute to think. Try to get each person to make a one- or two-sentence statement about how he or she will apply the lesson. What you're looking for is the take-away value—that which they'll remember after they've forgotten the rest of the lesson. I always try to include an "Aha!" in each lesson—that is, a new thought that revolutionizes our understanding of that passage.

Since these final thoughts may be the most important part of the discussion, it's important to allow enough time for summary and application before moving on.

Another alternative is to combine the disclosure time with summary and application. This will work particularly well if you've agreed in advance to limit prayer needs to applying the lessons of the discussion. People will already have been sharing needs throughout the discussion. It's relatively easy, then, to move to application in the form of prayer requests.

A form of question that we haven't discussed is the challenge question, which can take one of two forms. In either case, its purpose is to encourage group members to dig deeper and think creatively about the lesson.

Challenge questions tend to be memorable. That is, they continue to play back through the mind for the next week or so. And because they are of an entirely different nature than the rest of the discussion they put the subconscious mind to work and can often result in incredible gains in understanding or application even after the study is over.

The most common type of challenge question is often called "digging deeper," and is available in some study guides. These questions may require the use of various outside resources. They challenge the truly interested student to do a more thorough investigation of the subject. They often look more closely at the historical or cultural context.

To be most effective, a "digging deeper" type of question should end in application. For example, in studying the book of Joshua, such a question might be, "Research the religion of the Canaanites around 1400 B.C. How was this religion similar to beliefs expressed in the media today? How was it different?" Note that the "digging deeper" questions in many study guides will end after the first sentence. Stimulate your group by adding a modern-day application. And don't be afraid to discuss "digging deeper" challenge questions in your group if they're pertinent to your direction. People really will grow when they share on this level.

A much less common challenge question is what I call the "what-if challenge." In fact, although I often use them, I've never seen one in a study or leaders' guide! I love these because they really put the subconscious to work. I ask this type of question at the very end of the time together—even after prayer. I don't want people to answer it in the group. I want them to dwell on it all week. The following week, I may ask if anyone had any particularly interesting insights.

Let me give you a couple of examples of "what-if challenge" questions. You'll need to create them if you want to use them. In studying the account of the prodigal son it's common to ask which character each person in a group identifies with. This exercise gives you and your group insight into the needs and hidden motivations of each member. But you can go even further. At the end of one such study I asked, "Did anyone identify with the fatted calf? Think about how the fatted calf felt about the son's return, and apply that to your life."

In studying Matthew 4:18-20, where Peter leaves everything and follows Jesus, we often talk about what it cost Peter to make this decision. A challenge question might be, "What if you were Peter's wife or teenage son? How would you feel? What would you do?" That brings out a whole new area of consideration— one where someone else has made a decision that will intimately impact you. It hits home with a lot of people!

True, these challenge questions don't always yield a great new theological insight. Then again, sometimes they do! I've often found my understanding of a passage revolutionized by internalizing such a challenge question. They're simply another means of breaking through the conscious barriers that each of us employs for safety.

Asking Good Questions

✳

"'How can this be?' Nicodemus asked" (John 3:9)

Good discussions depend on good questions. If you can ask stimulating questions your group will enjoy a lively discussion and, as a result, will remember the main points far better than if you ask boring questions.

Here are some guidelines I use. First, a good question is clear. Either you can understand the question on the first reading or you can't. If you have to read a question several times before you "get it," chances are it's not a very clear question. When leading a discussion, rephrase any questions from the study guide that you think are unclear.

A good question is relevant. This goes back to your goal. Does this question move the study toward the goal? There are lots of theologically interesting questions, but so what? Will this question lead to a clearer understanding of the passage?

When deciding if a question is relevant you also need to ask yourself if your group has enough information to answer it. This may relate to the spiritual maturity of the group. If your group is composed primarily of young Christians they probably won't have the storehouse of understanding to answer some questions. More mature Christians can draw on previous knowledge, putting it together with what's in a given lesson to answer a question.

Relevancy may also relate to where you are in the study. We need to build precept upon precept. We need to be careful not to come out of left field with a question for which we haven't yet laid the foundation. Watch the flow of your questions.

A good question stimulates discussion. As we've said before, observation questions usually don't stimulate discussion. They're useful for background in personal study, but in the discussion you need to move quickly to interpretation and application questions.

Phrase your questions to avoid a "yes," "no," or a one-word answer. Questions that begin with "who," "what," "when," or "where" often result in one-word answers. Rather, ask "What do you think?" or "Why . . . ?" or "How . . . ?" These require people to get involved to turn their information into analysis.

Avoid questions that have only one "right answer." Leave room for the Holy Spirit to speak to each person. Encourage a diversity of responses. Phrase your questions so they offer several people an opportunity to respond. Discussion stimulates understanding and application.

It's fine to ask controversial questions. Don't be afraid if the discussion becomes heated. It's OK to

> "Do not pray for easy lives. Pray to be stronger men. Do not pray for tasks equal to your powers. Pray for powers equal to your tasks."
> —Phillips Brooks

raise the blood pressure a bit as long as people don't become offensive or hurt the feelings of others.

Phrase your questions so they are not too hypothetical, and so they lead to personal involvement. But be sure that no question will embarrass any group member or anyone else. If a group member wants to use himself as an example that's fine. But don't use him or anyone else—even your spouse or child— without their permission.

Finally, remember that not every discussion must end in agreement. That's hard for most of us to accept. We want to wrap it all up nicely and have everyone smiling as they leave. But sometimes the Holy Spirit does His best work when we leave a question unresolved at the end of a meeting.

Finishing Well

✳

"Teach us to number our days aright, that we may gain a heart of wisdom" (Psalm 90:12)

One of the most difficult tasks of the facilitator is that of keeping the group on time. It's a two-edged sword. If you're doing a good job people will be having such a good time in the discussion that they won't want to quit. If you're not facilitating well they'll be glad to finish early.

You will already have planned how long to devote to each element of your time together. Here are some suggestions for keeping the meeting flowing smoothly.

First, manage questions so everyone has an opportunity to participate. In most groups there are those who love to talk, those who'd rather not talk, and maybe a few in between. The easiest course is to let the talkers carry the discussion, but that's not fair to everyone else. If people truly remember best that which they have said, everyone needs a chance to talk, and it's your job to give it to them.

Make sure you allow enough time for summary and application. The amount of time you take will depend on the nature of the study. But as the facilitator it will be useful for you to draw the discussion to a logical end by making a summary comment.

And by all means, end the discussion in time to allow for sharing and praying. If your discussion is going well you may be inclined to let this part go. After all, everyone's enjoying it. But if you neglect time for sharing and praying you'll be cheating members out of an essential aspect of the group. And you may find that eventually discussions will falter or remain shallow because members don't really know or trust one another well enough to sustain the required level of intimacy in discussion.

The Importance of Evaluation
*

Once your group gets rolling, it's easy just to let it be. But I find it helpful to take the pulse of the group periodically. To do this I use various evaluation tools.

The first is the most informal and hopefully the most obvious. My co-leader and I try to stay in touch with the members and casually ask them how they're enjoying the group. What do they like? What don't they like? How can we make it more effective in their lives? If you show interest and are careful not to take offense at their comments, people are willing to tell you their needs. If you actually act on their suggestions, they'll begin to trust that you care about them and will tell you even more.

Second, after we've been meeting for a few weeks I do a short written evaluation with two or three questions. This allows the more reluctant members to give anonymous feedback. Usually I'll ask, "What two things do you like best about our group?" and, "What two things would you like to see improved?" It's short, simple, and takes five minutes. It says, "I care. Your opinions are important to me." If the group is continuing beyond 12 weeks, I may do this type of survey again when we're about two-thirds of the way through. For an ongoing group, I'll do it every few months.

Finally, at the end of the group or at the end of each study (usually 8 to 12 weeks), I do a more comprehensive evaluation. I ask for input on the quality of the study, the group's organization, the leaders and co-leaders, and anything else I want to know about. Most important, I commit myself to using this feedback to improve, either the next group I lead, or the remaining time with this group.

A sample of one final evaluation we've used is provided in Appendix E. Use this as a guide to develop your own. You'll note that we've used more "fill in the blank" or open-ended questions than multiple choice or ranking questions. We learn much more from the comments of the participants than from a raw score. It's easy to see why. A raw score tells you that they loved the study. A comment tells you why they loved it. That helps you make decisions for the next time.

We've also learned that if you want responses to written evaluations you must make time within your group. We've tried sending the evaluations home with people and have always been disappointed with the response rate.

"While all members are periodically involved in evaluating how the group is performing, the good leader will be constantly evaluating and taking corrective actions as necessary."
—Bob Parker, *Small Groups: Workable Wineskins*

CHAPTER 7

Why Didn't You Warn Me?

BY NOW, I hope that you have decided that leading a small group Bible study is definitely for you! I hope you've realized that you don't need the gift of teaching; that even you can facilitate a group. And I hope you've realized the tremendous growth and maturity that results from a good group.

It wouldn't be fair to leave you here, however. Lest you think it's all so simple, we need to discuss some problems that can occur in groups. In fact, I can almost guarantee you'll encounter at least one of these in each group you lead. In this final chapter I want to warn you of some potential problems and give you some pointers for handling them. If they don't catch you off guard you'll be able to take difficulties in stride and continue to enjoy leading your small group.

"I am not writing this to shame you, but to warn you, as my dear children" (1 Corinthians 4:14)

Let's look at a few of the most common areas that might cause you concern. I'll introduce you to a person, then discuss various ways to deal with his or her problem.

The Chronic Talker

✳

"When words are many, sin is not absent, but he who holds his tongue is wise" (Proverbs 10:19)

Mona Monopoly is a natural extrovert. She's also quite well-versed in Scripture and, in fact, has a lot of good points to make. The problem is that she makes them all the time! Every time you ask a question Mona jumps in with the answer before anyone else even has time to think about it. And her answers go on and on and on. You're finding that you can't get through the discussion you've planned because she's so long-winded. Others in the group have pretty much given up trying to answer a question. They simply watch you and Mona dialogue. What can you do?

Ask for short answers. Say, "In just one or two sentences, what do you think . . . ?" Be specific about the information you want and the fact that you want short answers. Do this often to reinforce your desire for brief answers.

Ask for several responses. Use this in combination with the above. For example, say, "I'd like several of you to comment on how you think . . ."

Call on someone else first. While I don't usually like to call on people, it may be necessary to break Mona's habit and give someone else a chance to speak. I'll do this several times, calling on various people, then call on Mona last.

Interrupt if necessary. We've all been admonished not to interrupt, but sometimes it's essential to give others a chance to answer. After Mona has made a couple of good points or when she begins to repeat herself, simply jump in and rather forcefully (but kindly) say, "Thanks, Mona. That's a great point. Jane, what do you think about . . ."

If Mona begins to ramble, again you need to be assertive. Interject by saying, "Wait a minute, Mona.

You're throwing out a lot of good ideas, but I'm afraid we'll lose track of them. Take one point, boil it down to one sentence, and let's see what the others think about it."

Talk to her. Find a time when you can meet with Mona privately in a casual, neutral setting. Affirm her and appeal to her desire to help you and the others. Be honest, but in a positive way. Say something like, "Mona, I really appreciate the way you always come with your homework done and with such good responses. I can tell that you're getting a lot out of this study. Now I need your help. Have you noticed that it takes some of the other members a bit longer to formulate their answers than it does you? When you jump right in with such thorough answers the others feel they don't have anything to add. I think they're a bit intimidated. I was wondering what would happen if you'd hold back a bit? Do you think maybe Jane or Karen would feel more comfortable answering?"

Ask her to help as a co-leader. Maybe Mona is being under-utilized. If she has most of the qualities of leadership, perhaps she is next year's leader. Ask her if she'd be willing to be a co-leader. If you already have a co-leader, what about an assistant co-leader? Affirm her. Work with her. Train her. Remind her that, as a co-leader, it's more important to encourage others to answer than to have the answer herself.

Use caution in this, however. Some Monas don't have the maturity to be a co-leader. They're using their skills at monopoly to cover their own insecurity or spiritual immaturity.

These techniques are hard. And sometimes they don't work because, even as leaders, we're reluctant to take charge. We don't want to appear too pushy or bossy. But sometimes it's necessary.

And of course, *pray for Mona.* As you pray for the various members of your group during your personal prayer time, pray that the Lord would show Mona how her behavior is affecting the group. Pray for her to be sensitive to the Holy Spirit, and allow Him to correct her talkativeness.

"He that cannot refrain from much speaking is like a city without walls."
—Sir Walter Raleigh

The Quiet Group

✳

"A time to be silent and a time to speak" (Ecclesiastes 3:7)

Perhaps you're facing the opposite of Mona. Perhaps your group responds to each question with a deafening silence. You ask a question, and after what seems like an eon no one has ventured a response. This problem is especially prevalent in a new group or in the first few minutes of a discussion. Now what?

Don't rush to fill the void. Sometimes, in our desire to be a great leader, we see silence as our enemy. Realize that you're better prepared than anyone else and you know where the discussion is going. Your group members don't. Remember that you already know the answer, as well as the next question.

Be sure to allow enough time for people to gather their thoughts and formulate an answer, especially for the first few questions of the day. Realize that they need time to hear the question, understand it, process it, find the answer in their study guide, decide if it makes sense in relation to the rest of the discussion, and open their mouths. That can easily take 15 to 20 seconds—longer if you've asked a question that's not straight from the study guide. But to you, 20 seconds feels like an eternity!

Time the silence. Glance at your watch when you ask the question. Don't panic until at least 30 seconds have passed.

What usually happens is that after 5 to 10 seconds the uncomfortable leader will rephrase the question or give the answer. That fills the silence and relieves everyone's distress. Rather, try letting the silence reign. Sit comfortably. Glance at a few people, but don't open your mouth. Before you know it the silence will make someone else uncomfortable and he or she will answer. Chances are, the discussion will be off and running.

Draw out quiet members. After you've allowed a reasonable silence, call on someone. Don't immediately zero in on the shiest or quietest member. Aim for the mid-range. Look for people whose eyes tell you they have an answer. Then smile and gently ask, "Tom, what do you think?"

If Tom says he doesn't know or passes, allow that. Try him again later, but allow him to maintain his dignity by not putting him on the spot.

Be sure your question is clear. Sometimes people don't answer because they don't understand the question, but they don't want to appear stupid by asking for clarification.

When preparing your lesson plan, be sure to test your questions against the guidelines in the previous chapter. If you think the question you've asked may be unclear, ask, "Does this question make sense?" or, "Maybe I didn't say that too well. Let me try again." Then rephrase the question. But the key is to use that as a last resort—not within the first 15 seconds. Once the group is comfortable with one another, someone will let you know if the question isn't clear.

> "Sometimes silence is not golden but yellow."
> —Wilbert Donald Gough

Answer in pairs. If you have a totally introverted group that regularly has a hard time answering in front of the whole group, try breaking them down into smaller, more comfortable groups. Divide people into groups of two and have them answer the question to each other. Next time, switch the groups around. Then break into groups of three or four. Gradually move into larger groups as people become more comfortable with one another.

Pray for your group, and for your understanding. In your personal prayer time, pray first that the Lord would show you what the barriers to discussion are in your group. Be willing to have Him show you any error you're making in leading the discussion. Then ask Him for specific wisdom in working with your group. You'll be amazed at what He shows you as you are faithful to pray!

The Silent Individual

❋

"Even a fool is thought wise if he keeps silent, and discerning if he holds his tongue" (Proverbs 17:28)

"One man keeps silence because he has nothing to say; another keeps silence because he knows it is the time for it."— Ecclesiasticus 20:6 (Goodspeed)

Your group as a whole is responding well, but Quentin Quiet never says a word. You know he's done his homework, but he's just not comfortable talking in front of the group. You don't want to ignore him, but you also don't want to push him. What can you do?

Spend some time with him outside of the group. Make a point of talking with Quentin before or after the group time. Chat with him during refreshments. Meet for lunch if you can. Let him see you as a friend. If you have a co-leader, encourage him or her to do the same. Then bring another person or two into that circle, perhaps during refreshments. Before long, Quentin may forget how shy he is and be comfortable enough to risk an answer.

Call on him. If Quentin was raised under the philosophy, "Children should be seen and not heard," maybe he's just waiting for you to give him "permission" to talk. Some people feel that what they have to say isn't very important, but if you ask their opinion, they'll give it.

Find a question you know he can answer or one that simply asks his opinion. Smile and say, "Quentin, what do you think about . . . ?" Give him time to formulate his answer. Affirm even the shortest and most hesitant response. But also give him the freedom to pass if he wishes.

Go around the circle. Find a question you'd like to concentrate on and go around the circle. Say, "I think this is an important question. Let's have everyone respond in just one or two sentences." Start at a point where Quentin won't be first or last, but a little past midway. You've reinforced that you want short answers so he doesn't have to give an oration. Affirm each response to build his self-confidence. You won't want to use this often, but once in awhile it may work to break down his barriers. If he passes, simply smile and move on. You don't want to put him on the spot.

Pray for Quentin. In your personal prayer time, pray that the Lord would give Quentin the same freedom to talk as the other members of your group have. Pray for wisdom to understand any specific barriers, including those caused by you or other members of the group.

Recognize that Quentin may be a truly wise person. Don't naturally assume that the quiet person isn't very smart.

The Person Who Won't Pray Aloud

*

"One day Jesus was praying in a certain place. When he finished, one of his disciples said to him, 'Lord, teach us to pray . . .'" (Luke 11:1)

Polly Prayerless contributes well to the group, but she simply won't pray aloud. In fact, before the first meeting she warned you that she wasn't one to pray in a group. There could be several reasons for this reluctance. Understanding them will help you encourage a person like Polly.

Praying aloud is new for many people, especially for new Christians. It's scary to hear your own voice talking to God. If your group includes new Christians or people whose religious tradition doesn't include audible prayer, be gentle and patient with them.

Others feel intimidated. Like Moses in Exodus 4:10, some feel that they're not eloquent enough to speak to God. They feel "slow of speech and tongue." This is particularly true when others in your group are eloquent and effortlessly pray on and on in the King's English. It's also common when there are wide educational differences among members of your group.

Some people are just naturally shy. It's not that they have anything against prayer. It's that they don't like talking aloud to anyone. They weigh every word and measure every sentence, but always feel they've come up short.

The key to handling any reluctant pray-er is sensitivity. We need to put ourselves in their shoes and not pressure them. What are some ways of doing this?

Let everyone know that they're under no compulsion to pray aloud. Before the first few prayer times, specifically state that you understand not everyone is comfortable with praying audibly. Affirm that their silent prayers are as effective as audible prayers, but that when they feel comfortable, they're welcome to join in. Assume that by the end of the group even Polly will be comfortable enough to pray aloud.

Encourage short sentence prayers. If you feel Polly is intimidated by the long-winded prayers of others, encourage everyone in the group to keep prayers brief and to the point. Do the same yourself. And allow Polly to pray silently for as long as she needs to.

Keep prayer conversational. While many people are only comfortable praying in King James English, others are terrified of making a mistake. If you have some in your group who always pray in a formal, stilted tone, break the mold by being contemporary, conversational, and even familiar.

Break into smaller groups for prayer. After Polly has become comfortable with the group in every other way, try breaking into groups of three for prayer. Let people choose their own partners or group Polly with the people she's closest to. Sometimes it's easier to break the silence with just a couple of close friends. Again, affirm each person's right to pray silently.

Don't go around the circle. If you do, Polly will spend the entire time in terror, counting the number of people until it's her turn. And the person after her, knowing of her reluctance, won't know whether to wait or to rescue her. If you see that prayer is beginning to go around the circle, jump in and pray out of turn to break it—even if you've already prayed once.

Don't call on Polly to open or to close in prayer. Ask for volunteers if you feel you need to assign certain positions.

Don't treat Polly differently from those who pray audibly. Let her know that she is loved and valuable just as she is.

Model prayers that reflect your honest feelings. If you're angry, don't tell God you're "bothered." Tell Him how furious you are. Be real and you'll be an encouragement to all of your group, but especially to Polly.

"He who has learned to pray has learned the greatest secret of a holy and a happy life."
—William Law

Pray for Polly. Pray privately for Polly to gain confidence. While audible prayer isn't the most important thing you'll accomplish in the group, it may make Polly feel better about herself. Often the people who are the most reluctant to pray out loud don't feel very good about who they are on other levels.

I've never yet seen this combination fail to produce a confident, outgoing person by the end of the group time together. And some of my most reluctant pray-ers have gone on to assume leadership in the next group!

The Person Who Doesn't Stay on Track

＊

"But the fruit of the Spirit is . . . self-control" (Galatians 5:22, 23)

Rhonda Rabbit is fun to have in your group. She's bright, witty, and quite intelligent. But it seems that no matter what question you ask she's suddenly taking the discussion off on a tangent. Sometimes you don't even realize this until it's miles from where you wanted to go. Her questions are always interesting, but they never go in the direction you had planned for that day. In a way she's like a hunting dog who catches the scent of a rabbit and is off chasing it instead of following the fox. How can you avoid going off on Rhonda's rabbit trails?

Be clear about your goal for the discussion. This is the main reason it's so important for you to have a goal or direction for the study. If you don't have a plan you won't realize until it's too late that the discussion is off on a tangent.

If Rhonda is in your group, it's especially important to communicate your goal clearly. Start the discussion by saying, "There were several interesting points in today's lesson, but the one I felt would be most beneficial for us to pursue is . . ." That puts everyone on notice that you'd rather not pursue the other "interesting points."

Take the subtle approach. Early in the group you may want to take an indirect approach. When you realize that Rhonda is chasing rabbits, let her finish, then redirect the question to another member of the group. Affirm Rhonda without encouraging her: "Thanks for that interesting point, Rhonda. Now, Chris, what do you think about . . . ?" This may be a good place to call on your co-leader, who shouldn't be intimidated by being called on.

Nip it as soon as you recognize it. You may need to progress to this strategy if Rhonda doesn't take the hint in your first couple of tries to get her back on track. As soon as you realize she's chasing rabbits again, interrupt and move the discussion back on track. You can affirm her by saying, "That's an interesting point, Rhonda. I wish we had more time to explore it. But I'm not sure I see how that relates to the question of . . ."

"If you don't know where you're going, any road will take you there."

By taking responsibility for your failure to see the connection, you don't embarrass Rhonda. You allow her to make the connection—if there is one. If there isn't, suggest that perhaps you can discuss her point after the meeting.

Pray for Rhonda. Most Rhondas aren't being malicious or trying to confuse you. There's a good chance Rhonda is scattered in every area of her life. Pray that she will see this as an area for growth. Pray for wisdom in helping her grow.

The "Super-spiritual" Person

✳

"A wise man's heart guides his mouth, and his lips promote instruction" (Proverbs 16:23)

Stanley Spiritual receives divine inspiration for every response. He prefaces each answer with, "The Lord told me . . ." The problem with this is that he may make the rest of the group feel as if he has a private line to God. The problem is compounded if he's theologically off base in his responses. How can you help Stanley?

Pray for discernment. Stan's responses could suggest one of several problems. If you can figure out which, you'll be better equipped to handle him. Pray for insight into his needs and his personality. Be open to the fact that perhaps he does listen more carefully and, in fact, does hear God. You'll know this by the quality of his answers. If they spring from a heart of wisdom you need only question his approach. If they spring from pride or insecurity, you need to deal more directly with him.

Talk about sensitivity. If you feel that his responses are generally good, try talking to Stanley privately. Ask questions that might give you additional insight into his needs or past experiences. Gently and lovingly let him know that his approach is getting in the way of people listening to him. Affirm him as a person. Let him know that you've noticed his wisdom. Encourage him to respond without always citing God.

> "Real spirituality always has an outcome."
> —Oswald J. Smith

Seek accountability. If you're certain that Stan's responses are not from God you still need to talk with him privately. Firmly insist that he not blame God for his lack of understanding. You can begin this process gently, but you may eventually need to be rather firm with him. If you feel that Stan is completely off base or causing confusion within your group, seek the assistance and wisdom of your minister or other church leaders.

The Dogmatic Person

✳

> "Let us therefore stop turning critical eyes on one another. If we must be critical, let us be critical of our own conduct and see that we do nothing to make a brother stumble or fall" (Romans 14:13, Phillips)

Donna Dogmatic is the first cousin of Stanley Spiritual. She's legalistic, dogmatic, and doesn't care whose toes she steps on. There's no hint of grace in her attitude. She pronounces her responses to questions with such a finality that no one dares suggest a different opinion. She has a copyright on the words "critical spirit." How can you offer constructive criticism to the person who's always right?

Pray for discernment. As with Stanley, your first task is to pray for wisdom and discernment. Donna's dogmatic approach and critical spirit could be a symptom of many problems. Perhaps she grew up in a very legalistic church or home and has never truly experienced grace. Perhaps she's covering up insecurity. Perhaps she's afraid to risk her shaky theology to the open discussion of others' opinions.

Begin with the indirect approach. When Donna

responds legalistically with her air of authority, don't be threatened. Smile and gently say, "That's an interesting point, Donna. What does someone else think about . . . ?" Call on your co-leader or another confident person if necessary. Gently try to suggest that, on many questions, there are several points of view.

Get direct if necessary. Legalism and dogmatism are like yeast that will ferment the entire group, especially when they're accompanied by a sharp tongue. If you aren't careful, someone will be hurt.

Find a time when you can talk with Donna privately. Affirm her as much as you can, especially for her firm stand on the essentials of the faith. Then suggest that not everything in the present study is an essential; that perhaps there are a variety of possible answers. Suggest that she's missing out on a wonderful opportunity to learn from the other members of the group. Add that they are also missing out on her wisdom because her tone often causes them to stop listening before she finishes.

Most of the Donnas I've known have not taken kindly to any suggestion of fallibility. I've seen groups deteriorate over insignificant issues. I've seen hurt feelings on all sides. But I've also seen a lot of grace ministered by others in the group. And I've seen several Donnas come back years later, grateful that we encouraged them to be more tolerant. I've seen some change their unbiblical positions and have prayed with others for release from a critical spirit or judgmental attitude.

This isn't an easy problem to face. But with prayer and grace, you may be able to moderate the negative effects of Donna.

Ask her to leave the group. One of my overriding principles of group leadership is that I won't sacrifice the group to minister to or contend with one person. This seems harsh, and it is. It took many years to reach this point and it's absolutely a last resort. I've only had to use it a couple of times. But a group is designed to minister to several people. If one person's needs, be-

> "It is ridiculous for any man to criticize the works of another if he has not distinguished himself by his own performance." —Joseph Addison

havior, or attitude is destroying the group, I must make a choice.

As much as I may want to help Donna, I have to put the health of the group above helping one person. If possible, I'll work with her outside the group. But I can't allow her yeast to ferment the others. When Donna's attitudes or behavior jeopardize the group, Donna must leave.

Peter Problem doesn't quite fit in. It took you a while to figure it out, but he really does have a serious emotional or psychological difficulty. He may suffer from undiagnosed or untreated paranoia, schizophrenia, depression, or any number of other disorders. The key for you is that his problem is manifesting itself in unacceptable ways and is disrupting the group. Of all the problems in this section, this is probably the most difficult for a lay person to deal with. So what do you do?

Pray for wisdom and insight. You may have initially identified Peter's problem as something else. You've already tried all the tips in that section and you're still baffled. If you haven't already, pray for wisdom in handling him.

Seek professional input. We're fortunate to have a psychologist in our congregation. Our church staff are also pretty good at recognizing when a problem is more than routine, and they're willing to get involved when we need them. If you're part of a small church or group where these skills aren't available, call around to other churches, particularly the larger ones, in your area. Or ask around to see if there's a Christian psychologist or psychiatrist in the area. Often these people will give you a few minutes of their time if you explain your problem. Or try your denomination's headquarters. We often used these outside resources in the San Francisco singles ministry before we had staff to turn to.

The Emotionally Disturbed Person

✳

"This day I call heaven and earth as witnesses against you that I have set before you life and death, blessings and curses. Now choose life, so that you and your children may live" (Deuteronomy 30:19)

Your goal in seeking professional help is to understand Peter and what he's dealing with. When you receive this help you'll learn what will help him and what will make his problem even worse. Not all psychological problems can be handled in the same way. In fact, an action that may be helpful for one problem can actually be harmful for another.

On the few occasions we've faced this problem, the lay leaders have been able to get a second opinion before taking any action. What we've found is that our Peter has also been causing similar problems in other ministries. Never have we been the first to bring him to the attention of the staff. Your discussion with these professionals will either confirm or change your own opinion and prepare you for the next step.

There are many excellent resources for your bookshelf or for your church library as well. Some of these are listed in the Appendix.

Try talking with Peter. Often Peter knows that he has a problem. Maybe he's even under treatment or on medication.

If he sees that you really care about him as a person and aren't going to condemn him, he may be willing to work with you. If so, consider developing a signal between the two of you so you can discreetly tell him that he's "doing it again" or he can tell you that he's feeling threatened or uncomfortable. Sometimes just having a friend who understands will be enough, particularly in the early stages of an illness.

Of course, you also run the risk that not only Peter, but also his family will deny that he has a problem. That's a much tougher problem that will probably require pastoral or professional assistance.

Spend a few minutes privately with Peter before each meeting. Try to get Peter to arrive a few minutes before the scheduled meeting time. Spend this time with him to check in and see how he's doing. You can also use this time to process any problems or needs that could exhibit themselves in the group setting if not dealt with. Consider this a time to help Peter reach his goals. If you can develop a strong personal relationship with Peter, you'll gain credibility in his eyes. His pleasure with your attention may result in your having enough influence in his life that you can work effectively with him.

Set firm guidelines. Whether he's faced his problem before or you're the first to point it out (which is unlikely if you've taken the above steps), Peter may react negatively. He may yell, deny, rationalize, threaten, cry, or otherwise try to intimidate you. However, the key, as we mentioned before, is that we can't allow one person to disrupt the entire group. You'll need to sit down with Peter and set firm behavioral guidelines, clearly spelling out what is and is not acceptable. At this point some Peters will voluntarily leave your group; others will agree to give it a try with the new rules.

Depending on your conversations with your ministers or other professionals, you should decide just what you will or won't accept before you ask Peter to leave the group.

If Peter's not already getting professional help, ask him if he's interested. If necessary, help him identify possible resources and funds. Then encourage him to make the initial calls and appointment. If he's apprehensive, offer to go with him the first time to help soothe his fears or shyness.

Ask him to leave the group. As always this is the last resort, but it's an action you must take if Peter's behavior is interfering with the ability of the rest of the group members to grow. Try to offer an alternative. If you feel you can handle it, offer to continue meeting privately. If not, suggest that he get professional help and give him several telephone numbers. Follow up even after he leaves. It's especially important in this case not to let him feel abandoned. Don't just leave him to flounder unless that's his choice.

"There is a tendency among Christians to assume that all abnormal behavior is caused by some spiritual problem. Certainly it's true that emotional break-downs often do result from one's spiritual condition, but to suggest this as the only explanation is a gross oversimplification. . . . The conclusion reached by almost all . . . researchers is that the causes of abnormal behavior are varied and extremely complex."
—Gary R. Collins, Ph.D., *Fractured Personalities*

The Bored Person

✻

"The backslider gets bored with himself; the godly man's life is exciting" (Proverbs 14:14, *The Living Bible*).

Yolanda Yawner is always bored. You can see it in her eyes. You can hear it in her yawns. You know it for sure when she pulls her nail file out and starts doing her nails. You're not sure why she's here, but she sure doesn't contribute much.

Do a "boring" check. Maybe your group is boring. Before you get too upset with Yolanda be sure that the group warrants her attention. Perhaps, as in the women's group I mentioned earlier, the study is lethal. Perhaps the people have no interest in it. Perhaps your questions or your tone lack an attitude of interest or excitement.

Privately ask others what they think of the group. Ask Yolanda if she's bored. Find out what you might do to make it more interesting. If she has a valid complaint, you'll all benefit from making the necessary changes.

Pray for insight. As with so many of the preceding problems, take this one to the One who knows why Yolanda's behaving as she is. Pray for a heart of wisdom and insight. Pray for gentleness and graciousness as you work with her.

Try to figure out why she's reacting like this. This attitude is most common in a high school group where the student couldn't care less about the group, but Mom insists she attend. Even if Yolanda is an adult this may be a carry-over from adolescent behavior.

It may be that Yolanda is backsliding or grappling with a major spiritual issue. It may be that she is hurting deeply and puts on the bored veneer to keep you and everyone else out. Or it may be that Yolanda simply doesn't realize the message her behavior is communicating.

Talk to Yolanda. After you think you understand why she's acting like this, pray for grace, then find time to talk with Yolanda privately. You may need to schedule lunch or a walk in the park after church. You want enough privacy and time to be able to serve her.

Begin the conversation lovingly and gently. Avoid any hint of anger or malice. After appropriate small talk you might say, "Yolanda, I've noticed that you seem to be a bit bored by the group. I'm wondering if there's anything I can do to help you enjoy it more."

Maybe she'll respond; maybe she won't. Maybe she'll hit you with both barrels. If so, her charges may or may not be valid. Maintain your composure. Listen with your heart as well as your head. Don't accept all of the blame, but also don't fight back. Let her know that you love her and want to help her in any way you can. Ask for her help in creating a more positive atmosphere in the group.

"When people are bored, it is primarily with their own selves that they are bored." —Eric Hoffer

Take it to the group. If your talk with Yolanda yields no change and you feel it's still a problem, test your concern with a trusted member or two. Be careful not to turn this into a gossip session. Simply ask for their help and their ideas. If others are as concerned or bothered as you are you will need to take it to the group. At the beginning of your next meeting open by saying, "I've become concerned about what appears to be lack of attention or an attitude of boredom within the group. I want our group to work together, but I don't feel we can if everyone isn't functioning at about the same level of enthusiasm. How are you feeling about it?" This conversation will be easier if there are several problems you can address, such as people coming late or leaving early, irregular attendance, and people not doing their homework.

If Yolanda feels singled out, she'll either be very quiet, hoping to fade into the upholstery, or she'll react with anger. Be prepared for both. Ultimately, the group will need to set some guidelines that everyone agrees to abide by. You may want to introduce the group covenant if you haven't done so already.

The Person Who Doesn't Understand

✳

"Who can discern his errors? Forgive my hidden faults" (Psalm 19:12)

Willy Wrong seldom has the right answer—even if the question has several possible answers. Sometimes it's as if he answers a different question than you ask. Maybe he's just slow. Maybe he doesn't listen well. He's not trying to be funny, but sometimes it ends up that way. After all, how could anyone come up with the answers he does? You hate to embarrass the guy, but what can you do?

Pray for discernment. There could be many reasons for Willy's problems. Pray for wisdom to identify just why he is always so far off base. That will help you to deal sensitively with him.

Offer to study with him. If Willy seems genuinely concerned and wants to do well in the group, offer to study with him a time or two. That may help you understand where he's going wrong. Does he read or hear well enough to understand the questions? Does he appear to have some sort of learning disability or neurological problem? If so, is he aware of his problem, and is he getting help? Are there ways you can help him?

Affirm him even while correcting. Whether or not you can get to the source of the problem, don't embarrass him. If he gives a wrong answer (and Willy usually isn't shy, so he will), smile and say, "That's an interesting perspective, Willy. Ted, what do you think?"

Again, here's a good place to use your co-leader. You can be sure he or she won't make a snide remark about Willy's answer.

"One must never confuse error and the person who errs."
—Pope John XXIII

Linda Lazy and Buddy Busy have similar problems. They seldom do their homework. Linda just isn't interested, and Buddy can't seem to fit it into his 60-item to-do list. The problem is that this format of group discussion works best when everyone prepares. If the group is expecting you to teach them and you're expecting them to share from what they've learned in their own personal study, you've got a problem! How do you handle it?

Remind everyone of the need to do their homework. Particularly if this type of group is new to your members, you may need to remind them that you aren't going to teach the lesson. If no one does the homework the discussion will flounder. Make this reminder gently and frequently at the beginning or end of the group time. Hopefully you'll break a bad habit before it starts. This will be easier to do if the group has agreed, either verbally or in a covenant, to be faithful in doing their homework.

However, I also tell my group members that I want them to come even if they haven't done their homework. Most people can benefit from the discussion even if they haven't studied the lesson, and I believe that the continuity of the group is more important than doing one's homework. Not everyone agrees with me here.

Ignore it. If I only have one or two such people in an otherwise conscientious group, I must confess that I often simply ignore it unless Linda or Buddy begin causing problems by their lack of preparation. I've found that they usually won't volunteer an answer they don't know, and sometimes the frustration of being unprepared will motivate them. I know that simply showing up is an effort for many people, and I try to give a little grace whenever possible.

The Person Who Won't Study

✳

"A sluggard does not plow in season; so at harvest time he looks but finds nothing" (Proverbs 20:4)

If the disease begins to spread to others who think, "If Linda can get away with not doing her homework, I can too," I'll take a more definitive action.

Refuse to allow participation. This is the technique used by the very successful Bible Study Fellowship organization. If you don't do your homework you're welcome to sit in on the discussion, but you can't talk. It's effective, and offers an incentive for most people to try a little harder to schedule time for the homework.

Re-evaluate the workload. If several people are having a hard time getting their homework done, you may want to re-evaluate the workload. The studies in some series take about two hours to do. That doesn't seem like much, but it may overwhelm many busy executives or homemakers.

To lighten the workload in our Moms' Bible Study, we took two weeks for each lesson. The first week we went through the entire lesson. The second week we specifically applied that lesson to our roles as wives and mothers. Meanwhile, the women could begin the next lesson, giving them two weeks to do it. Surely anyone can find an hour a week to study the Bible!

A little every day. Encourage everyone to spend some time each day working on the lesson rather than leaving it until the night before your group meeting. This has two advantages. First it will get them into the Word every day—a worthy goal in itself! And second, it will prevent the problem of their having nothing done when something else comes up the night before.

Pray for your group, and especially these members. It's hard to find time to do a Bible study lesson, particularly if it's a new addition to your schedule. Pray that it will become such a priority for each person that he or she will find the time somewhere. Also recognize that this may be the work of the Enemy in Linda or Buddy's life. Satan will do almost anything to keep God's people out of God's Word. Laziness and busyness are two great excuses! Some aggressive spiritual warfare may be called for.

> "Beware of squatting lazily before God instead of putting up a glorious fight so that you may lay hold of His strength."
> —Oswald Chambers, *My Utmost for His Highest*

Clancy Cliché has a well-worn answer for everything. He's full of jargon, especially Christianese, and seldom conveys much of anything. He's quick to offer a pious non-answer, but you can't get him to delve deeply enough beneath the surface to respond with a meaningful answer. He always has advice for people with prayer requests, and it's usually something like, "Just trust and obey and everything will turn out OK." You wish you could hide behind the nearest bush! How can you reach Clancy?

Ask for clarification. Especially if Clancy grew up in the church, he may have cut his teeth on phrases like "saved by the blood," "justification," "the throne of grace," and "propitiation." Maybe he knows what they mean; maybe he doesn't. The best way to find out is to ask for clarification. Say, "Could you expand a bit more on that, Clancy? How does taking our requests to the throne of grace apply to this question?" or, "When you say we're justified by faith, what does that mean to you?"

You may need to ask several follow-up questions before you get an answer that most of the group understands. This may seem tedious, but you're also modeling the type of answer you want. Hopefully as the group goes on, Clancy and all the members will respond with more definitive answers.

Explain why it's important to give concrete responses. The whole group may need to understand why you continue to probe when someone responds with jargon or a cliché. Say, "You may wonder why I ask for clarification on so many responses. It's because I really want to make sure that we are all understanding one another. Sometimes when we give an answer that's too familiar, different people understand it in different ways. I want to be sure that we understand each answer in the context of our discussion."

The Person Who Uses Jargon

*

"But I tell you that men will have to give account on the day of judgment for every careless word they have spoken" (Matthew 12:36)

"One great use of words is to hide our thoughts." —Voltaire

Encourage prayer rather than answers. When Clancy gives his "trust and obey" response, you need to remind the group that we aren't here to solve problems or even respond to the prayer needs. We are simply here to pray. Of course you'll want to do this for everyone, not just for Clancy.

Pray for Clancy. In this situation I'd pray first for wisdom and insight into why Clancy uses so much jargon. Maybe he's never learned to articulate, but maybe he's got a deeper problem he's hiding. Only the Holy Spirit will be able to give you the wisdom, insight, and gentleness you'll need.

The Person Who Has Multiple Problems

✳

"I have told you these things, so that in me you may have peace. In this world you will have trouble. But take heart! I have overcome the world" (John 16:33)

If Dora Dither didn't have bad luck, she wouldn't have any. She tries so hard to be faithful to attend the group, but her three little ones always seem to be sick. And when she's there she consumes the group with her needs. Her husband hasn't earned enough for the family to live on for months. Last week he left her and the children. She doesn't know where he is. Her mother just had a heart attack and her frail father is helpless without his wife around. Dora's youngest was just diagnosed with leukemia, and Dora's migraine headaches are back.

You think I'm exaggerating, but I can almost guarantee you that, if Dora isn't in your group this time, she will be next time. Some people seem to have a monopoly on misfortune—and they need your group. The problem is, they're so needy that you may feel ill-equipped to deal with them, and everyone else feels embarrassed to share what they consider comparatively minor needs. How can you handle this touchy situation?

Encourage group members to spend special time with Dora. She needs all the support you can give her. She needs friends to stand by her, bring her meals, supply a bag of groceries, baby-sit sick children, and just listen. There will be people in your group who are particularly drawn to her, or who have the gift of mercy. Privately encourage them to do whatever they can to help her or just be with her. Call her during the week to check in and to pray with her.

Provide material assistance. Encourage Dora by helping out where you can, especially anonymously. One of my great joys has been to see how the women in our various Bible study groups have taken the initiative to come through for our Doras. I've seen women spontaneously organize a grocery drive where dozens of bags of food and household products "mysteriously" appear one morning. I've known of several Doras finding fifty-dollar bills in their purses or hundred-dollar bills in their mailboxes. This is truly the body of Christ at work, and it will solidify your group as few other things will.

Allow Dora to share first. If your group is feeling overwhelmed, and members are unwilling to share what they consider to be more minor needs, you need to intervene. As needy as Dora is, others also have valid needs that you won't want to ignore.

Ask Dora to give her update first. Limit her time to something reasonable by saying, "Dora, can you take just five minutes and update us on how we can pray for you?" At the end of the five minutes, gently interrupt and suggest that the group stop and pray for her right now. Take whatever time the group needs to pray. This will affirm Dora and will give her the recognition that her needs require without ignoring everyone else. It will also create some space between her sharing and that of the other members, which will lend some objectivity.

After prayer, move on to the others. Give them whatever time they require. Then pray for those needs.

Just one need. If you're short on time, if Dora's needs have made a habit of overwhelming the group, or if she repeats the same story every week, change your practice for a week or so. Instead of being open for all prayer needs ask, "What one thing can we pray

> "Obstacles are those terrifying things we see when we take our eyes off our God."— Anonymous

about for you this week?" Give members a minute to isolate their most important need, then share and pray accordingly.

Pray for her. It's obvious that Dora's greatest need is for prayer—constant, consistent, committed prayer. Make it your practice to pray for Dora every day. Encourage others in your group to do the same. Then stand back and watch God work. Dora's circumstances may not change, but I can almost guarantee you that her outlook will!

The Argumentative Person

✳

"As charcoal to embers and as wood to fire, so is a quarrelsome man for kindling strife" (Proverbs 26:21)

Arthur Argumentative loves a good "discussion." He doesn't see what he's doing as being argumentative. He just enjoys a lively exchange. The problem is that his aggressive nature offends or scares the other members. Sometimes he even gets a little personal, calling the responses of others "dumb" or "crazy."

Note that we're not talking here about a lively, spirited discussion. That's our goal! People will get a bit excited if they're engrossed in a challenging discussion. That's what we want. But Arthur has moved beyond lively and spirited. He's downright rude. How can you deal with someone who steps over the line from discussion to argument?

Pray for him. As with so many of these problems, it's important to take time to regularly and fervently pray, both for Arthur and for your wisdom in handling him. Ask the Lord to show you what might be behind Arthur's belligerence, or at least to give you the wisdom to do no harm as you deal with him.

Clarify the ground rules. If Arthur's attitude isn't posing an immediate problem, wait until the beginning of the next meeting to clarify how you expect group members to relate to one another. This takes the heat off of Arthur and redefines the ground rules for everyone.

Firmly stop the argument. If the indirect approach doesn't work—and it may not—you need to be more assertive in stopping Arthur as soon as he begins to become argumentative. Begin gently, but increase the firmness until he catches on.

You might begin by repeating your ground rules in a firmer manner. For example, say, "Let's remember to consider one another's feelings as we discuss this." If that doesn't stop him, next time be more direct. "Arthur, I know that you feel strongly about your position, but you simply may not insult other members of the group. Can you rephrase your comment in a way that respects the opinions of others?" I'm always reluctant to embarrass members, but sometimes there's no other choice if I'm considering the good of the group as a whole.

Talk privately with Arthur. As soon as possible after confronting him in the group, you need to speak privately with Arthur. Schedule lunch, or find another time when you can have a fairly extended time with him. Let him know that his attitude is causing division among the other members. See if you can agree on some new ways for him to respond. If he seems genuinely interested in improving his behavior, you may want to meet together several times. Continue working with him as long as you see progress and a willingness on his part to try to change, and as long as he doesn't adversely affect the life of the group.

Ask him to leave the group. This is absolutely the last resort, but on rare occasions it's necessary. By the time we get to this point it's usually a mutual decision. Again my standard is that I will not sacrifice the group for the sake of one individual, especially if that individual won't follow with commonly accepted group norms. Some people are simply not at a point in their lives where they can benefit from a group, and the group is seldom a place of rehabilitation for such people. Therefore, don't allow them to destroy the group.

> "People generally quarrel because they cannot argue."
> —G.K. Chesterton

The Person Who Gossips

✳

"A gossip betrays a confidence, but a trustworthy man keeps a secret" (Proverbs 11:13)

Griselda Gossip can't help herself. Every time someone in the group discloses a deep personal need, Griselda finds someone else to share it with. She doesn't do this maliciously. Sometimes she's simply sharing a prayer request that isn't hers to share. When the word gets back to the group members they stop sharing and the group begins to lose its vitality. What's the solution?

Clarify the ground rules. As soon as you find out about the first breach of confidentiality remind the group members of how you expect them to handle anything they hear in the group. Go over the rules of confidentiality again. If you've signed a group covenant, remind members of the confidentiality clause. Don't name any names at this point unless the gossip has already started a wildfire. Give Griselda the benefit of the doubt—once.

Firmly intercept the gossip at the earliest possible point. If the indirect approach doesn't work—and it may not—you need to be more assertive in stopping Griselda as soon as you learn of the gossip. Begin gently, but increase the firmness until she catches on.

You may want to find a time you can meet privately with her. Begin by repeating the ground rules in a firmer manner. For example, say, "Let's remember that none of us has any right to share anything we hear in the group. Anything disclosed belongs to the sharer."

If that doesn't stop her, next time be more direct. "Griselda, I know that you don't mean to hurt anyone by sharing their prayer needs. In fact, you probably feel that you're helping them. But you simply may not disclose any information you get in this group. If this continues, we'll have to ask you to leave the group."

You may also need to remind Griselda that gossip, even with the best of intentions, is a sin. Take time to point out some of the scriptural admonitions to tame the tongue, such as James 3:2-12, Proverbs 11:13, 16:28, 20:19, and 2 Corinthians 12:20.

Pray for her. You need to begin praying as soon as you first get wind that someone is gossiping. When Griselda is identified you need to pray for her, and pray for wisdom in dealing with her and with your group. Depending on her attitude, this can be a minor bump or a huge mountain in the development of trust in your group.

Apply Matthew 18 to the situation. If Griselda doesn't accept that gossip is a sin you may need to apply Matthew 18:15-17 to the situation. Take another member of the group—perhaps your co-leader—and meet with Griselda. Approach her with an attitude of love and respect after having prayed diligently for wisdom. Tell her that you are coming in the spirit of Matthew 18. Read the passage to her. Remind her of any specific instances of gossip you know of. Try to verify if these are true if there's even the slightest doubt that you've heard the whole story. Give her an opportunity to repent. If she refuses to acknowledge her sin, you'll need to proceed with the next step.

Ask her to leave the group. This is absolutely the last resort, but you've warned Griselda of the consequences of her actions. You can't sacrifice the group for the sake of one individual. Even at this point it will take some effort on your part to restore the confidence of the group.

"The tongue is the measure of the spiritual life of the man . . . if we are truly mature and under the control of God, then our tongues will reveal that fact. When God has bridled the entire life, then the tongue is bridled. Thus, when the tongue is bridled it is an indicator of the measure of Lordship Christ is exercising in our members."
—David H. Roper,*The Law That Sets You Free*

The Unrepentant Person

❊

"No one who is born of God will continue to sin. . . . This is how we know who the children of God are and who the children of the devil are: Anyone who does not do what is right is not a child of God . . ."
(1 John 3:9, 10)

Sydney Sinner is living a life that's clearly sinful in some area. Maybe he's living with his girlfriend or you learn that he's engaging in fornication or adultery. Maybe, like Griselda, he talks too much. The list of potential sins is too long to list, but you know them, and they're affecting your group. This is among the most difficult problems to deal with because it requires excellent discernment. What's your role in the situation?

Pray for wisdom. We're all sinners. If we're looking for a perfect group filled with sinless people we'll never find it this side of Heaven. So first you need to pray for wisdom and tolerance.

You need to evaluate prayerfully why you believe Sydney's sin is a problem to the group. You need to decide if he's chosen a life-style of sin, as opposed to the isolated sins that we all commit.

Sydney's sin will probably be one of "those" sins. You know, the sexual sins—adultery, fornication, homosexuality. For some reason we seem to think that God puts them in an entirely separate category. Before we do anything at all, we need to be confident of His opinion about the sinful life-style we see.

Evaluate the action needed. The action you need to take will depend on why you believe Sydney's sin is a unique problem. Is he flaunting it? Is it affecting others in the group? Is it so public that it compromises the integrity of others in the group? You need to be clear on why you want to deal with Sydney's sin and not anyone else's. You can be sure that Sydney will question your motives.

Most sins can be dealt with gently and gradually during the course of the group. And in fact, that's usually the best choice. As people begin to trust one another, they'll also be more receptive to correction. Once we've lost a person to the group we've also lost our best opportunity to influence or minister to him. So if the sin isn't affecting the life of the group or causing someone in the group to stumble, I prefer to work privately with Sydney for as long as possible.

Talk privately with Sydney. Find a time you can talk privately and at length. Lovingly and gently tell him what you've heard or seen. You might say, "Sydney, we haven't known each other for long. I've really come to admire you, but I'm concerned for you. I understand that you and Gloria have moved in together. Is that true?"

Give him a chance to explain, but be alert for the excuses, the justification, or the anger that may follow. Be open to the possibility that your information was inaccurate, exaggerated, or another person's bitter accusation. Since you will already have clarified your position biblically, try pointing out appropriate passages that relate to his situation. Point out 1 John 3:9, 10, which calls Sydney's commitment to Christ into question.

"The object of love is to serve, not to win."
—Woodrow Wilson

Apply Matthew 18. If Sydney refuses to change his life-style, you may need to apply Matthew 18. As with Griselda, take another person with you to try again. This may be your co-leader, your minister, a deacon, or an elder. Discuss the sin and why it is a problem both for Sydney and for the group.

Ask Sydney to leave the group. If Sydney refuses to repent or change his behavior you'll need to ask him to leave the group. Always try to leave the door open to continue meeting privately or to serve him in any way you can. Your goal is not to be right—it's to restore him lovingly (see Galatians 6:1).

The most difficult situation I ever faced in this area was when as a co-leader I needed to confront the sin of the leader shortly after the beginning of a group we had planned for months. It left me in an awkward position. It was one of the most difficult actions I've ever had to take. But it was the right decision.

The Non-Christian

✳

"This is good, and pleases God our Savior, who wants all men to be saved and to come to a knowledge of the truth" (1 Timothy 2:3, 4).

Suzy Separate is not one of us. You thought she was when she joined the group. She certainly talked a good game. But as time goes on, it's clear that she doesn't have a personal relationship with Jesus Christ, nor does she accept the authority of the Bible. And to make matters worse, she asks tough questions that appear not to have answers! Now what?

Pray, pray, pray. More than anything you can say or do, prayer is absolutely the key with Suzy. Pray that she'll be open to the wooing of the Holy Spirit. Pray that you and your group will be sensitive to her. Pray that you'll be part of the solution rather than part of the problem. And pray that the Enemy will be defeated. You can be sure that the closer Suzy draws to Christ the hotter the warfare will be. Suzy won't know what's going on but you will. So before doing anything, pray.

Offer her love and acceptance. If Suzy is truly seeking truth we want to help her in any way we can. That means loving her, talking with her, sharing the gospel with her, and giving her time. If she's not disrupting the group, don't push or rush her. Allow the Holy Spirit to draw her to himself.

Spend time with her. Be sure to make time outside of the group to talk with her. Have fun together. Answer any questions you can. And most important of all, simply continue loving her. Encourage others in the group to do the same. You'd be amazed to learn how many seekers have become Christians through the loving consistency of fellow group members.

Answer those questions that aren't disruptive. While I'd be the last person to put a serious question about salvation on hold, use discernment in leading your group. Suzy probably has more questions than you can answer in your group time. Her understanding of the Bible is limited enough that many of her questions will lead to chasing rabbits. And if you answer all of her questions you'll find that you have a group devoted to Suzy.

Therefore, you may need to suggest politely that you'd be happy to answer that question during refreshments, but that to do so now would lead the group too far off the subject. Then make a note of her question so you're sure to bring it up at the appropriate time.

Find someone who will meet with her privately. If Suzy is truly seeking God, she'll welcome the offer of someone to study with or to have lunch with. If you can't do it yourself find someone in the group who is willing to spend time answering her questions. That should limit the time in the group devoted to her. Again, we don't want to sacrifice the group for one person, especially if that one person can be better served individually.

"Our task as laymen is to live our personal communion with Christ with such intensity as to make it contagious."
—Paul Tournier

The Cult Member

*

"Dear friends, do not believe every spirit, but test the spirits to see whether they are from God . . ."
(1 John 4:1)

Claude Cult has no interest in your Bible study—other than to lead its members away to his cult. Yes, there are cults that are known for infiltrating and destroying Christian groups. Their members are well-versed in Scripture, and you may find yourself rejoicing at having such a knowledgeable person in your group. But beware. These cults talk about Jesus, but they don't know Him or serve Him. And they will devour the lambs if you aren't careful. What do you do if you find yourself in such a situation?

Listen with discernment. If you have someone in your group you don't know, pray for discernment as you lead the group. Pray that if there is anything unpleasing to the Lord, He'll reveal it to you. I've been amazed at how quickly we've been able to discern a disruptive spirit in the group. Sometimes I've spotted it—other times someone else has. There's never been a consistent give-away. But the Lord has always been faithful in showing us quickly.

Clarify the motive. I'm always a little hesitant to move too quickly in this situation, but it's one where indecision can be lethal. As soon as there is any sign that a person may not be attending with pure motives you need to confront him. If you're unconvinced by his explanation, offer to meet privately with him. Bring along someone who is more knowledgeable than you.

Ask him to leave. This is tough but essential. You must be firm and unequivocal. As a minister told our singles group the first time we faced a group of infiltrators from a cult, "Our first responsibility is to protect the lambs." Unless your group is made up of mature Bible scholars who love a challenge, you're better off inviting the cult member to leave.

He may tell you that he really wants to learn more about Jesus. He's sure to tell you how bigoted, discriminatory, and narrow-minded you are. But your first responsibility is to protect the flock God has entrusted to you. Don't play with fire; get rid of cults quickly and forcefully.

> See the Appendix for several resources on cults.

> "What we should read is not words, but the man behind it."
> —Samuel Butler

Dealing With Conflict Among Members

✳

> "'In your anger do not sin:' Do not let the sun go down while you are still angry, and do not give the devil a foothold" (Ephesians 4:26, 27)

Connie Conflict and Annie Anger are neighbors. They hate one another. No one is quite sure when the animosity began, although there are lots of stories. Each of them joined the group without knowing that the other was also joining. Now you have open warfare on your hands. Each has steadfastly declared that she won't leave and let the other win. What can you do?

What else? Pray. As much as you want peace to reign in your group, it's unlikely to occur without some concerted prayer. And even with prayer, you may lose one or both of these members. You need to pray for wisdom and discernment.

Try to take action. Should you try to get them together to talk? You can try, but don't be surprised if one or both are unwilling. Should you allow one or both of them to quit the group? You probably don't have much choice. Should you decide who's to stay and who's to go? Never! Should you talk privately with each and point out the sin of their anger? Absolutely!

You may also try putting them in separate small groups if yours is a large Bible study. That will reduce, but not eliminate, their interaction. Or perhaps you know of another small group one of them might bene-fit from. While you'd prefer to end the warfare, you may be most effective if you can work with one or both of them privately.

Don't allow the fight to polarize your group. If both women decide to stay in the group (and that's unlikely in the long run), you can't allow their argument to polarize the group or create an uncomfortable air. You need to talk with each separately and be very clear about the ground rules. If the feud continues, treat them as unrepentant individuals continuing in sin. Whatever you do, you must stay in control.

"In battle those who are most afraid are always in most danger."
—Catiline

The End —and the Beginning...

WE'VE COME A long way! We started with an idea —leading a small group Bible study—and have looked in detail at every step along the way. Perhaps by now you're feeling quite overwhelmed. I can assure you, however, that if you've made it this far, you've learned a lot about small groups.

And now you're equipped to do an excellent job leading one. Don't worry that you can't remember everything. Keep this book on hand and use it whenever you have a question. Review it often as a refresher for your personal maturity as a leader.

And more than this book, you have the Holy Spirit —the Spirit of the Living Lord—who has promised to guide you. Commit your group to Him, and He will bless it, and you, abundantly.

"And my God will meet all your needs according to his glorious riches in Christ Jesus" (Philippians 4:19)

So go ahead. Give it a try. Call your minister or some friends and start a small group Bible study. You'll never be the same again!

And when your first group ends, let us know how it went. Let us know where you were prepared and where you weren't prepared. Let us know how we can improve this handbook so it will remain a useful tool for you.

And may the God who led a small group of twelve men in Galilee so many years ago also lead you.

"The multitudes can be won easily if they are just given leaders to follow."
—Robert E. Coleman, *The Master Plan of Evangelism*

APPENDIX

Resources for Leaders

THE FOLLOWING ARE some of the resources you may want to use as you lead your group. Begin to collect them as you can afford them—or check your church library.

Bibles

*

Study Bible

A good study Bible is essential to any Bible study leader. A study Bible will include comprehensive study helps such as marginal notes, footnotes, topical study outlines, historical information, and much more. Be sure to use a good translation, rather than a paraphrase. Experts disagree on which translation has the best scholarship, but you will seldom go wrong using the *New American Standard Bible* (NASB), the *New International Version* (NIV), or the King James Version (KJV). Better yet, cross check all three. Here are some of my favorites:

Thompson Chain Reference, New International Version
Zondervan Bible Publishers, 1983
Grand Rapids, MI

Master Study Bible (NASB and KJV)
Holman Bible Publishers
Nashville, TN

Parallel Bible
A parallel Bible includes the complete Bible in four (or more) translations in parallel format columns. It is particularly useful for gaining a more rounded understanding of a difficult passage as you read it worded in several different ways. This format makes comparison of translations much easier than balancing four or more separate Bibles! I recommend my favorites.

The Layman's Parallel Bible
Zondervan Bible Publishers, 1976
Grand Rapids, MI

Includes the Old and New Testaments in the King James Version, *Modern Language Bible, Living Bible, Revised Standard Version*

The Four Translation New Testament
World Wide Publications 1966
Minneapolis, MN

Includes the New Testament only in King James Version, *New American Standard Bible,* Williams, and Beck.

Small Group Bible

The NIV Serendipity Bible for Groups
Zondervan Publishing House, 1989
Grand Rapids, MI

This NIV Bible compiled by Lyman Coleman and his "Serendipity" group is an excellent resource if the study guide you've selected has weak questions. Designed for small groups, it provides questions for every passage in the Bible, both Old Testament and New. Although they name them differently, these questions include the four types discussed in this handbook—icebreakers, observation, interpretation, and application. (The same authors also have a New Testament-only version available, called The Serendipity Bible Study Book.)

Bible Dictionary

A Bible dictionary actually serves as both a dictionary and an encyclopedia. It provides historical and cultural information and defines and clarifies names of persons, places, and objects to which the Bible refers. It usually includes information on each book of the Bible (author,purpose, form, origin) and some maps. Two of the many excellent ones include:

New Unger's Bible Dictionary
Moody Press
Chicago, IL

Zondervan Pictorial Bible Dictionary
Zondervan Publishing House
Grand Rapid, MI

**Bible
Reference
Materials**

✳

Concordance

A concordance lists alphabetically every word in the Bible, along with the reference where it is found. It is useful for two main purposes: to locate text by knowing only a few words, and to identify the Hebrew or Greek word used and to learn the meanings and roots of those words.

Hebrew and Greek dictionaries are available at the back to further define each word. You can select a concordance for each translation you use regularly, as well as the original King James Version.

For many years, the industry standard has been *Strong's Exhaustive Concordance of the Bible,* published by various publishers. Almost all concordances use Strong's numbering system—important if you expect to use many other reference works. In fall 1990, Zondervan published *The NIV Exhaustive Concordance,* which is expected to become the new standard. It also uses Strong's numbering system.

Expository Dictionary

An expository dictionary provides an alphabetical listing of major words in the Bible translated into English (from KJV), with the various Greek words and definitions of those words for each. It often discusses cultural meanings, roots, or other information to give a fuller understanding of words. The standard is

An Expository Dictionary of New Testament Words
Fleming H. Revell Company, 1966
Old Tappan, NJ

Bible Handbook

Bible handbooks are all different, but they provide a wealth of information. Some have historical and cultural information, some are mini-commentaries.

Select one or more that provide the information you need most often. I use

Halley's Bible Handbook
Zondervan Publishing House, 1965
Grand Rapids, MI

Unger's Bible Handbook
Moody Press, 1972
Chicago, IL

Blaiklock's Handbook to the Bible
Fleming H. Revell Company 1980
Old Tappan, NJ

Bagster's Bible Handbook
Fleming H. Revell Company, 1983
Old Tappan, NJ

This last is my favorite—a virtual gold mine in 245 pages.

Bible Atlas

Bible atlases provide maps, information on Bible places, and historical, geographical, and cultural background. They're very useful in many types of study. Several companies have excellent atlases. Look around for one that provides the information you want.

Commentaries

Bible commentaries come in all shapes, sizes, and quality. Some are one volume—others include many volumes. Each includes an analysis of Bible passages that help you to better understand what you're reading. Get a good one-volume commentary, then supplement as you are able with a multi-volume set. Try to balance the theological perspectives of the different authors so you can gain the best understanding.

Greek and Hebrew Word Study References
Most small-group Bible study leaders don't know Greek or Hebrew, but the following are references that will help you do word studies. I highly recommend these resources.

The Word Study New Testament and The Word Study Concordance
George V. Wigram and Ralph D. Winter
William Carey Library, 1978
Pasadena, CA

The Word Study New Testament provides an interlinear numerical reference to each word or phrase of the New Testament. This reference is keyed to the companion *Word Study Concordance* and to Strong's Concordance. *The Word Study Concordance* then lists every time the Greek word is used in the New Testament, with additional keys to other Greek lexicons and study books.

The advantage of this system is that many Greek words are translated into more than one English word in the Bible. If you don't know this, using Strong's alone will give you only a limited view of the word. This concordance shows every instance the Greek word is used and how it is translated in each verse. It also leads the reader to root words for further study.

Theological Dictionary of the New Testament, Abridged in One Volume
by Geoffrey W. Bromiley
Gerhard Kittel and Gerhard Friedrich, Editors
William B. Eerdmans Publishing Company, 1985
Grand Rapids, MI

This is the one volume version of the multi-volume "Kittel" your minister probably uses. But one volume is enough for most of us! This book provides excellent discussions and expanded definitions of Greek words used in the New Testament, including use in secular

Greek, the Septuagint, rabbinic literature, and various biblical uses. It provides a comprehensive understanding of Greek words for the lay leader.

Theological Wordbook of the Old Testament
R. Laird Harris, Gleason L. Archer, and Bruce K.
  Waltke
Moody Press, 1980
Chicago, IL

This is about the only Hebrew word study book I've found for the person who doesn't know Hebrew. It includes definitions of words used in the Old Testament, keyed to Strong's numbering system. It references a long list of other books and provides bibliographies where necessary. It's not as "user friendly" as the Greek helps listed above, but it's better than the alternatives.

Hermeneutics Books
These books will give you a good understanding of Bible interpretation. Most are written for the lay reader.

Understanding the Scriptures
Hans Finzel
Victor Books, 1988
Wheaton, IL

Designed like a workbook, this text is advertised as "a fresh, new look at inductive Bible study." It provides an excellent understanding of the how's and why's of Bible study and is aimed at the lay reader. You could use this book to lead a small group study on how to study the Bible!

How to Read the Bible for All It's Worth
Douglas Stewart and Gordon Fee
Zondervan Publishing House, 1982
Grand Rapids, MI

This is an excellent, non-technical introduction to hermeneutics for lay people.

Keys to Understanding and Teaching Your Bible
Thomas E. Fountain
Thomas Nelson Publishers 1983
Nashville, TN

A mid-level book that addresses 22 keys to understanding Scripture. It provides a good description of the grammatico-historical method, then discusses the various special categories of biblical literature (allegories, parables, types, poetry, and more).

Toward an Exegetical Theology: Biblical Exegesis for Preaching and Teaching
Walter C. Kaiser, Jr.
Baker Book House, 1981
Grand Rapids, MI

A professional level book that coined the "syntactical-theological method." This book includes discussions of contextual, syntactical, verbal, theological, and homiletical analyses, as well as the use of prophecy, narrative, and poetry in preaching. Excellent, but heavy, reading.

Other Resources
✳

Small Group Resources

The Master Plan of Evangelism
Robert E. Coleman
Fleming H. Revell Company, 1973
Old Tappan, NJ

Although this book is not specifically on small group leadership, it is must reading for leaders of small groups. Coleman uses Jesus' work with the Twelve as our model for making disciples.

Small Group Evangelism: A Training Program for Reaching Out with the Gospel
Richard Peace
Inter-Varsity Press, 1985
Downers Grove, IL

A training program to use small groups for personal evangelism. Includes a good discussion on group dynamics.

Growth Through Groups
William Clemmons and Harvey Hester
Broadman Press, 1974
Nashville, TN

This book approaches groups from the perspective of personal and corporate growth in three areas: growth in *koinonia,* growth in depth, and growth in mission.

Getting Together: A Guide for Good Groups
Em Griffin
Inter-Varsity Press, 1982
Downers Grove, IL

This is an excellent book on group dynamics, but since it's written at the college level, it takes a real commitment to read it.

Leading Bible Discussions
James F. Nyquist and Jack Kuhatschek
Inter-Varsity Press, 1985
Downers Grove, IL

A 64-page primer on starting and leading a small group Bible study. This book provides an excellent overview of the important issues in small groups, although there is almost no detail.

How to Lead Small Group Bible Studies
The Navigators
Navpress, 1988
Colorado Springs, CO

Another excellent but short primer on starting and leading small group Bible studies.

Using the Bible in Small Groups
Roberta Hestenes
The Westminster Press, 1983
Philadelphia, PA

The comprehensive text on small groups by one of the nation's acknowledged experts. Unfortunately the layout and format of the book make it almost unapproachable. (If you have difficulty finding this book, Westminster Press has merged with John Knox Press and is now in Louisville, KY.)

Good Things Come in Small Groups: The Dynamics of Good Group Life
Written by a small group consisting of Steve Barker, Judy Johnson, Rob Malone, Ron Nicholas (coordinator), and Doug Whallon
Inter-Varsity Press, 1985
Downers Grove, IL

This is an excellent, readable handbook on small groups. A must for every leader's library.

Psychology

Resources for Christian Counseling
Gary R. Collins, Ph.D.
Word, Inc.
Waco, TX

This is a series of individual books, each one dealing with a specific psychological problem.

They're useful for an intensive look at an individual problem once it's been diagnosed.

Fractured Personalities
Gary Collins, Ph. D.
Creation House, 1972
Carol Stream, IL

This book was written from an evangelical perspective for pastors to show them how to use psychology in the church. The author discusses the nature of emotional disturbance—what causes it, what kinds of symptoms will be seen and what types of treatment and professional help are available.

Christian Counseling
Gary Collins, Ph.D.
Word, Inc. 1988
Waco, TX

An exhaustive encyclopedia of emotional problems. Perhaps one of the best.

Cults

Spiritual Counterfeits Project
P.O. Box 4308
Berkeley, CA 94704
(415) 540-5767

For the most recent and comprehensive details on cults and the New Age movement, contact this research and information organization. Author Tal Brooke is the director.

The Mind Benders: A Look at Current Cults
Jack Sparks
Thomas Nelson Inc. Publishers, 1977
Nashville, TN

This book provides a comprehensive look at three "Eastern" or Hindu cults (Transcendental Meditation, Divine Light Mission, and Hare Krishna) and four "Western" or "Christian" cults (The Unification Church of Sun Myung Moon, The Children of God, The Way International, and The Local Church of Witness Lee). Although it's old, it still has good information.

When the World Will Be As One
Tal Brooke
Harvest House Publishers, Inc. 1989
Eugene, OR

This book exposes the New World Order of the New Age movement. It's an excellent resources for evangelizing people involved in the New Age movement.

Riders of the Cosmic Circuit
Tal Brooke
Lion Publishing Corp., 1986
Batavia, IL

A look at some of the newer Eastern religions.

Kingdom of the Cults
Walter Martin
Bethany House Publishers, 1985
Minneapolis, MN

This is a scholarly look at the beliefs of a number of cults.

Worship

Hymns for the Family of God
Paragon Associates, 1976
Nashville, TN

This hymnal is an excellent resource for small group worship. It includes traditional hymns, some of the older popular choruses, poetry, and responsive readings.

Praise Chorus Book
Maranatha! Music (distributed by Word, Inc.)
Waco, TX

Available in music book and words-only edition, this book contains a large selection of the Maranatha praise and worship choruses and a few familiar hymns. It's a versatile and affordable resource for your group.

Come and Worship
Michael Coleman and Ed Lindquist
Chosen Books, 1987

This book discusses the healing power of worship and the ministry of the Integrity Hosanna music company.

APPENDIX B

Sample Get-Acquainted Openers

The key in planning openers and ice-breakers for your new group is to keep them light and non-threatening, but having the potential for depth. It's a delicate balance, but here are a few I like. The key is to begin to set the stage for self-disclosure and transparency.

Wallet Scavenger Hunt

This is absolutely my favorite get-acquainted exercise because it offers so much flexibility. People can share deeply or on a surface level, as they choose. Regardless, you learn a lot about everyone in a short time. This opener is adapted from "Serendipity" material by Lyman Coleman.

Instructions: Have each person go through his or her wallet and/or purse. (If you have a mixed group, limit to the wallet only to keep it fair for the men.) Find and share briefly something that

1. I've had a long time
2. I like to do
3. I'm very proud of
4. Reveals a lot about me
5. Reminds me of a beautiful experience
6. Gives me concern/worry
7. I prize the most

Group Inventory

This is also adapted from "Serendipity" material by Lyman Coleman. Do this individually or in pairs.

Have each person or team calculate the total of these items, then elaborate briefly:

___ different states you've lived in
___ houses you have lived in
___ different high schools you attended
___ pictures of boys or men you have with you
___ pictures of girls or women you have with you
___ love letters you have with you
___ speeding tickets you've ever received
     (minus 5 points each)

Open-ended Questions

Ask one or more open-ended questions. But realize that even some of these questions may open an old wound. Listen with your heart. Go around the circle with one question, or give members their choice of three pre-selected questions to answer. Limit responses to 2-3 minutes and keep the discussion moving.

1. Something unique about my first job.
2. One thing I've never tried, but would like to.
3. The best thing that happened to me today.
4. On my day off I enjoy . . .
5. Complete the phrase, "I am . . ." seven different ways.
6. My favorite room in the house is . . .
7. If I could change my vocation, I'd like to be . . .
8. I feel like . . . (select an animal, then tell why)
9. If I could pick one character in a book, a TV show, or a movie to identify with, it would be . . . (Why?)
10. The most frightening experience I ever had.
11. The most influential person in my life (besides Christ).
12. The two most valuable possessions I have. Why are they valuable?
13. Where I lived and what I did when I was in the sixth grade.

APPENDIX C

Small Group Bible Study Covenant

Small Group Bible Study Covenant

Group Leader _____ Phone _____

Group Co-leader _____ Phone _____

We exist for growth in spiritual maturity through

Scripture   For each member to grow in knowledge and application of the Word of God.

Worship   For the group to bring joy to our Lord through praise, thanksgiving, and prayer.

Relationships   For each member to develop deep and abiding personal relationships in an atmosphere of acceptance and accountability.

Ministry   For each member to develop the mindset of a servant and to use his or her spiritual gifts to build up the body of Christ.

Expectations

Attendance
1)   We will meet together every week/every other week (circle one) on (day of week) _____.
2)   Our commitment to this group will last from (dates) _____ to _____.

3) Our meetings will begin at (time) _____ and close at
    _____.

4) We agree to be faithful in attendance and to call someone in the
    group if we cannot attend.

Scripture

1) We will study _____.

2) We agree to complete the study guides to the best of our ability.
    Yes ___ No ___.

3) We agree to take part in the discussions, sharing what we have
    learned in our study and learning from the insights of others.
    Yes ___ No ___.

4) During the meetings, our study will last approximately (how long)
    _____.

Worship

1) The primary way(s) our group will express worship to God is
    _____.

2) We agree that our worship time will last approximately (how long)
    _____.

Mission

1) The primary purpose of our group is _____
    _____.

2) We will seek to take part in some ministry as a group (service
    project, other). Yes ___ No ___.

3) In what ways will spiritual gifts be developed, encouraged, and
    used toward those within the group and those outside?
    _____.

Community, Transparency, and Accountability

1) Will our group be open to having new members join?
    Yes ___ No ___

2) The primary ways our group will seek to build openness and
    accountability are: _____
    _____.

3)   The amount of time given for sharing or disclosure will be approximately (how long) _____.

4)   How will refreshments be handled? _____

5)   We will have time for informal conversation before or after meeting (How long? When?) _____.

Prayer

1)   The amount of time devoted to prayer within the group will be approximately (how long?) _____.

2)   Prayer in the group setting (will ___ will not ___) be limited to specific needs.
If so, define:_____

Other

1)   Children over the age of _____ (will ___ will not ___) attend the meetings.

2)   How will child care be handled? _____
_____.

3)   At the end of our group commitment, we will complete an evaluation(Yes ____ No ____)

We agree together to honor this group covenant.

_____

Member's signature

Adapted from Community Group Leaders' Training Manual, Central Peninsula Church, by Mark Mitchell, 1987.

APPENDIX D

Lesson Plan

Lesson Plan

Use this form to plan each group session. Adapt it as necessary. You may want to type it on larger sheets of paper and photocopy it for ease of use.

Text: _____

Title: _____

Summary or Principle:

Goal:

Setting the Direction:

Launching Question:

Notes:

Maintaining the Direction

Section 1 (Title) _____
Question:
Question:
Question:
Notes:

Section 2 (Title) _____

Question:
Question:
Question:
Notes:

Section 3 (Title) _____

Question:
Question:
Question:
Notes:

Summary and Application

Summary:
Application:
Challenge:
Assignment:
Notes:

Adapted from Community Group Leaders' Training Manual, Central
Peninsula Church, by Mark Mitchell, 1987.

APPENDIX E

Bible Study Evaluations

Bible Study Evaluation

This evaluation is designed to help your leaders improve the structure, design, and presentation of future studies and meetings. We would appreciate your honest evaluation. Please pray before you answer the questions, asking the Lord to give you wisdom as you communicate your concerns.

Rating System E = Excellent, G = Good, F = Fair P = Poor

Material/Topic

1. The study on Joshua spoke to my personal needs.   E G F P
2. The study helped me identify and conquer
   giants in my spiritual life.   E G F P
3. I will continue to apply what I have learned
   to my daily life.   E G F P
4. The questions in the study were clear and
   understandable.   E G F P
5. I found the lessons challenging and enjoyable.   E G F P
6. I would recommend this study on Joshua to
   other Christians.   E G F P

Specifically, what did you like about this study?

Specifically, what did you dislike about this study?

What changes have you seen in your life as a result of this study?

These evaluation forms are samples for you to examine. Use them as models to compile customized forms for your group.

Additional comments, thoughts and suggestions

Interaction with others in the group:

1. How did you like the size and age mix of your group?

2. Did you feel at ease contributing to discussions and sharing your concerns? If not, how could this be improved?

3. Do you have any suggestions on improving the study or prayer time?

4. Are there any other ways group interaction could be improved?

5. Rank in order of importance the elements of the group in your life (#1 being the most important):
   Bible Study ____   Fellowship ____   Prayer ____

Statistical Information:

1. Please check one:
   Single ____ Married ____ Divorced ____ Separated ____ Other ____

2. Age Range:
   20-29 ____ 30-39 ____ 40-49 ____ 50+ ____

3. How long have you been a Christian? ____

4. Do you also attend another Bible study? ____

Leadership Evaluation

Please do not sign your name.

Leader's Name _____ Co-leader's Name _____

Rating system (check one for each column):
E = Excellent   G = Good   F = Fair   P = Poor

		Leader	Co-leader
1.	My leaders were well prepared and showed a solid knowledge of the Bible.	E G F P	E G F P
2.	My leader was able to organize and utilize his her time efficiently so that we rarely ran late (answer only for leader).	E G F P	
3.	There was a good balance between study time, prayer, and sharing.	E G F P	E G F P
4.	My leaders were understanding, sympathetic, and helpful when special personal struggles were shared.	E G F P	E G F P
5.	My leaders demonstrated the ability to pray effectively.	E G F P	E G F P

6. My leaders were able to show
   transparency (honesty) in sharing
   their own lives with the group.   E G F P   E G F P

7. My leaders were conscientious in
   following up on absentees.   E G F P   E G F P

Please share what you appreciated most about your leader and co-leader.

Leader:

Co-leader:

Additional comments, thoughts, suggestions for improvement

APPENDIX F

Permissions

Chambers, Oswald. *My Utmost for His Highest*. Dodd, Mead, & Company, New York. Copyright © 1935 by Dodd, Mead, and Company.

Clemmons, William. *Growth Through Groups*. (Nashville: Broadman Press 1974). All rights reserved. Used by permission.

Coleman, Robert E. *The Master Plan of EVANGELISM*. Fleming H. Revell Company, Old Tappan, New Jersey. Copyright © 1963, 1964 by Robert E. Coleman. Used by permission.

Evans, Louis H. Jr. *Covenant to Care*. Victor Books, Wheaton, IL. Copyright © 1977 by Louis H. Evans, Jr. Used by permission.

Griffin, Em. *Getting Together: A Guide for Good Groups*. InterVarsity Press, Downers Grove, IL. Copyright © 1982 by Inter-Varsity Christian Fellowship of the United States of America.

Hansel, Tim. *You Gotta Keep Dancin'*. David C. Cook Publishing Co., Elgin, IL, page 41. Copyright © 1985 by Tim Hansel. Used by permission. Available at your local Christian bookstore.

Hestenes, Roberta. *Using the Bible in Groups*. The Westminster Press, Philadelphia, PA. Copyright © 1983 by Roberta Hestenes.

A Navigator Guide: *How to Lead Small Group Bible Studies*. NavPress, Colorado Springs, CO, pages 9 and 14. Copyright © 1982 by NavPress. Used by permission.

Parker, Bob. *Small Groups: Workable Wineskins*. Christian Information Committee (now Equipping Ministries

International), Cincinnati, OH. Copyright © 1988 by Christian Information Committee. Used by permission.

Richards, Lawrence O. and Gib Martin. *A Theology of Personal Ministry* (retitled *Lay Ministry* in 1988). Copyright © 1981 by The Zondervan Corporation. Used by permission.

Nicholas, Ron, et. al. *Good Things Come in Small Groups.* Copyright © 1985 by Inter-Varsity Christian Fellowship of the United States of America. Used by permission of InterVarsity Press, P.O. Box 1400, Downers Grove, IL 60515.

Sweeten, Gary, Ed.D. *Apples of Gold II: Speaking the Truth in Love.* Christian Information Committee (now Equipping Ministries International), Cincinnati, OH. Copyright © 1987 by Christian Information Committee. Used by permission.

Sweeten, Gary, Ed.D. *Breaking Free From the Past.* Christian Information Committee (now Equipping Ministries International), Cincinnati, OH. Copyright © 1980 by Christian Information Committee. Used by permission.

Index